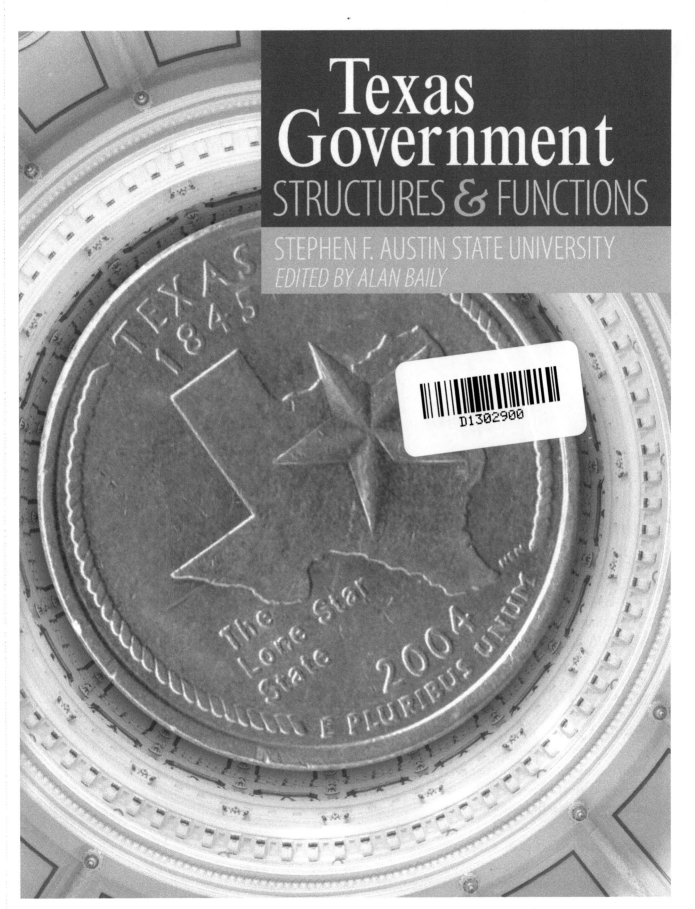

Texas Government
STRUCTURES & FUNCTIONS

STEPHEN F. AUSTIN STATE UNIVERSITY
EDITED BY ALAN BAILY

Kendall Hunt
publishing company

www.kendallhunt.com
Send all inquiries to:
4050 Westmark Drive
Dubuque, IA 52004-1840

CONTENTS

CHAPTER 1

The Texas Legislature

Dr. Donald M. Gooch

A Sea Change in Texas Partisan Politics in the State Legislature

The Texas Legislature is the dominant political branch of state government under the Texas Constitution's separation-of-powers institutional arrangement. A legislature is the lawmaking body of a governmental unit, and it is traditionally viewed as the most important institution of government. A legislature has the power to enact, amend, and repeal the laws that govern public policy. One of the most important legislative roles is that of developing and amending the budget, which is the plan for government spending in a fiscal year. In addition to lawmaking, a legislature serves as a check on executive power through its oversight and investigative powers, it serves as the primary representative body in the government, giving effect to the views and preferences of the citizenry, and has the power of the purse—the authority to tax, spend, and borrow money for public purposes. Members of a legislature are called legislators, who are elected from geographic districts to represent the electorates of those districts in a seat in the legislative body. Legislatures can be unicameral, consisting of one chamber, or bicameral, consisting of an upper and lower chamber of representatives that separately deliberate and vote on laws. The Texas Legislature is the governmental institution in Texas with the primary responsibility for writing bills and passing laws. It exercises plenary powers for writing and approving bills that may become laws. It is the constitutional successor to the Congress of the Republic of Texas, which was the legislative body for the Republic of Texas before Texas joined the Union and became a state in 1845.

The Texas Legislature is often the backdrop for partisan politics in Texas. This has become even more common in the wake of the fundamental shift in Texans' partisan affiliations over the past few decades. Texas voters, along with the rest of the states in the formerly Democratic "Solid South," have increasingly favored the Republican Party. While the inflection point for this change in party preferences dates to seismic shifts in the national electoral coalitions of the two major political parties in the 1960s and 1970s, this new partisan dynamic was slow to emerge in state and local elections in the South. For a time, Democrats in the South were able to blunt the electoral effects of the shift in public sentiment towards the Republican Party through localized campaigns, gerrymandering, and strong party organization. In Texas, Democrats were able to maintain control of the state legislative branch through the 1990s. But for the first time in 130 years, the Republican Party elected a majority of their members to the House and Senate, gaining full control of the Texas Legislature starting in 2003 from the Democrats.

An example illustrating the lawmaking and political power of the Texas Legislature, as well as the seismic shift in the partisan makeup of the institution, can be found in the mid-decade redistricting controversy of 2003. One of the important institutional roles of state legislatures in our federal system under the US Constitution is their primary responsibility for drawing the districts from which representatives are elected to the US House of Representatives. **Gerrymandering** is redistricting (drawing districts) for partisan advantage. Partisan gerrymandering has been ruled constitutional by the Supreme Court, and both political parties tend to partisan gerrymander when they control a state's legislature. Generally, redistricting occurs in the year following the national census, which occurs decennially (every ten years). Texas Democrats, through their generational control of the Texas state legislature, had gerrymandered the districts in Texas such that they were able to maintain a majority of the Texas US House of Representatives' seats despite the sea change in Texas electoral politics in favor of the Republicans throughout the 1980s and 1990s. In 2001, Democrats and Republicans were unable to agree on new district maps. Thus, per the Texas Constitution, the Legislative Redistricting Board convened and created a new redistricting plan. The LRB creates a redistricting plan only when the Texas state legislature is unable to pass a redistricting plan. In June 2001, the LRB approved a new map which maintained the 17-to-15 Democratic majority in the US House delegation from Texas.

Control of the state legislature having passed to the Republicans in 2002, the Republicans in the state legislature, in close collaboration with Republican House Majority Leader and Texas Representative to the US House of Representatives, Tom Delay, introduced a measure in the state legislature to redraw the judicial districts from 2001. While redistricting usually occurs concurrent with the national census, federal courts ruled that a mid-decade redistricting was constitutional. Unable to stop the plan from passing in the legislature, fifty-two Democratic members of the state legislature fled the state to prevent a quorum in the Texas State House. A **quorum** is the minimum number of members of a legislative body necessary to have present during a session in order to act officially (i.e., pass legislation). These Democrats, nicknamed the "Killer Ds," returned to the state when Republicans promised them the redistricting plan would not be introduced in a regular session. However, Governor Rick Perry called a **special legislative session** in order to reintroduce the redistricting plan. After Democrats effectively thwarted the redistricting plan in that special session by invoking a two-thirds rule, a legislative rule that required a supermajority to pass the plan, Governor Perry called another special session. This spurred eleven Democratic senators to flee the state and once again deny the Republicans a quorum to pass the plan. After a stand-off that went on for more than a month, Democratic Senator John Whitmire returned to the State Senate, and the redistricting plan was passed in a third special legislative session. With the new districts in place for the 2004 elections, the Republicans won a majority of the Texas US House seats for the first time since Reconstruction, twenty-one seats to eleven seats.

The political gambits state legislators played with institutional and representational rules in squaring off in the 2003 redistricting fight are emblematic of modern Texas state legislative politics. This snapshot of partisan rancor, recrimination, and retribution is no anomaly—it is a function of the colossal shift in Texas partisan politics that has culminated in the Texas political environment we see today. As we will see, the Texas legislature has become more ideologically polarized, more partisan, and more hierarchical in the modern era. Ideological polarization redounds to a more confrontational style of legislative politics, as we saw in 2003. Furthermore, the redistricting controversy underlines the important and perpetual debates over the nature of representation in electoral institutions and the recursive, strange loops that can sometimes produce major changes in the political landscape. Seemingly small, inconsequential shifts in local and state politics can reverberate and aggregate at the national level and on a national scale. It also demonstrates the central importance of the state legislature as a focal point for policy change and how institutions and the ossified procedural rules that constitute them can be manipulated strategically to serve or thwart electoral and institutional majorities.

Texas State Legislature: Basics and Comparison to US Congress

The Texas state legislature, like most state legislatures in the United States, is closely modeled off of the US Congress. Table 1.1 presents a side-by-side comparison of the Senate and the House of Representatives for the US Congress with the Texas State House and the Texas State Senate. The structure of the Texas state legislature clearly echoes that of the federal legislature. Both institutions are bicameral: they are composed of a lower house and an upper house. In both institutions, the lower chamber is called the House and the upper chamber is called the Senate. Senators serve longer terms than do representatives of the lower house and their terms are staggered (only a portion of the Senate is up for election in any given election year). Just like the US Senate, you have to be older to serve in the Texas Senate than you do in the House, and Texas senators serve larger geographic regions and populations than do the representatives to the House. In the case of both legislative institutions, you must be a resident of the state in order to represent that state in the legislature. The hierarchical organization of the Texas State House and that of the US House of Representatives is similar to that of the US House of Representatives; with the leader of the respective bodies both called the Speaker of the House. Finally, the Texas state legislature's bill process is similar to that of the US Congress, which we will discuss in detail later in the chapter.

TABLE 1.1 Comparison of US Congress and Texas Legislature				
	US Congress		**Texas Legislature**	
Characteristic	**US Senate**	**US House**	**Texas Senate**	**Texas House**
Size of Chamber	100	435	31	150
Term in Office	6	2	4	2
Staggered Terms	YES	NO	YES	NO
Minimum Age for Election	30	25	26	21
Resident of State	YES	YES	5 years	2 years
Resident of District	N/A	NO	1 year	1 year
Terms	Annual	Annual	Biennial	Biennial
Presiding Officer	Vice President	Speaker of the House	Lieutenant Governor	Speaker of the House

While it should be evident that the federal and Texas legislatures have similar institutional designs, there are a few important differences between the two that bear mention. The most important of these differences is the periodicity of the legislative terms at the federal level versus that of

Texas. The US Congress meets annually in year-long sessions punctuated only by breaks for holidays and recesses so that representatives can return to their home states and interact with their constituents. The Texas state legislature, however, has a biennial term: it meets once every two years. The Texas Legislature meets in regular session on the second Tuesday in January of each odd-numbered year, per the Texas Constitution. Texas is only one of eight states that do not meet in annual sessions. Legislatures with biennial sessions tend to have lower rates of productivity, in terms of policy output, than do states with annual legislative sessions. Per the Texas Constitution, the Texas Legislature meets in regular session for 140 days every two years. The primary responsibility for a regular session is the setting of the state budget. Legislators may also introduce changes to Texas statutory and constitutional law. As noted in the discussion of the 2003 redistricting controversy, however, the governor may call **special sessions**. A special session of the legislature is for thirty days and the governor may determine the topic for the special session. For example, Governor Perry called the Texas state legislature into special session specifically to pass the redistricting plan. In off years, the Texas state legislature does not meet. Since budgeting and agency evaluation must occur annually, these responsibilities are vested in the Legislative Budget Board. Established in 1949, the LBB is a ten-member, permanent, joint policy-making board that oversees all state government agencies and includes the lieutenant governor, the Speaker of the House (who serve as chairman and vice chairman, respectively), two senators appointed by the lieutenant governor, two representatives appointed by the Speaker of the House, the chairmen of the Senate Finance and State Affairs committees, and the heads of the House Appropriations and Ways and Means committees. The board appoints the budget director and prepares the budgetary requests and appropriations bills for all state agencies for both regular and special sessions. Also, the LBB conducts program evaluation for state agency programs and operations, which are reported to the Texas state legislature.

Another significant structural difference between the US Congress and the Texas state legislature is the organization and leadership of the Senate. In the US Congress, the Senate is organized horizontally, with individual senators possessing a great deal of power in the legislative process. However, in the Texas State Senate, power is structured similar to that of the US House of Representatives and the Texas State House—it is structured vertically, with the leadership of the Senate exercising a great deal of control and authority over the legislative process. Thus, while the role of the vice president in the Senate is mostly symbolic, except when breaking tie votes, the role of the lieutenant governor in the Texas State Senate, as president of the Senate, is significant. Much like the Speaker of the House, the lieutenant governor has a great deal of influence over the legislative process in the Senate. The lieutenant governor establishes all special and standing committees, appoints all chairpersons and members, and assigns all legislation to the standing committees at will. Additional to his role on the Legislative Budget Board, the lieutenant governor is an *ex offico* member of the Texas Legislative Council, which is the legislature's research and investigative agency. He is also a member of the Legislative Redistricting Board, which, as noted earlier, is charged with adopting a redistricting plan for the federal and state districts in Texas if the legislature fails to do so or where the legislature's redistricting plan is ruled unconstitutional by a court of jurisdiction. The lieutenant governor's role in the Texas State Senate has led many observers of Texas politics to suggest that the lieutenant governor is more powerful than the governor in Texas.

There are other differences between the US Congress and the Texas state legislature, some more significant than others. Congress is considerably larger in size than the Texas state legislature. You have to be older to serve in both houses of Congress than you do the parallel houses in the Texas state legislature—four years older to serve in the US House (twenty-five years old) or Senate (thirty years old) than to serve in the Texas State House (twenty-one years old) or Senate (twenty-six years old) respectively. Unlike Congress, there is a one year district residency requirement to run for the Texas State House or Senate. And the terms in office differ for the upper houses. While the Texas state legislature mirrors the federal legislature in having the upper house members serve longer terms than that of the lower house and the lower house members serve two-year terms, Texas State Senators serve for four years, not six years like their federal counterparts. These differences may seem relatively minor, but taken as a whole they result in a federal legislature composed of older, more experienced members with greater institutional capacities to make laws and a larger reservoir of institutional knowledge than that of the Texas state legislature.

Representation and Structural Capacities in the Texas Legislature

What does **representation** mean? What does it mean to be represented, in the political context? As a form of government, representation took flight in the works of Enlightenment political philosophers in the seventeenth century, culminating in the United States, the first of the modern representative democracies. Enlightenment thinkers emphasized representation as essential to the new State because it would permit the formation of nations with diverse ethnicities, values, and beliefs. The etymological root derivation of "representation" is from the Latin, *repraesentare, representationem* or *repraesentatio*, meaning to "bring before, exhibit." But it also takes meaning from the Old French term *representacion,* "to portray," and the late Middle English definition of "representation" where it was understood to mean "image or likeness." Both root meanings have significance to our understanding of political representation. Political representatives are tasked with "bringing before" the seat of government the views, ideas, values, and beliefs of their constituents and "exhibiting" them within the legislative context. Furthermore, the concept of representative is intimately tied to the idea that the individuals representing others should mirror their constituents' "image or likeness" both in their political and policy preferences and in their personal characteristics. Both meanings of representation are important to understanding the role of political representatives in modern democratic politics.

According to political scientists, political representation is characterized by the following four components: (1) some party representing (i.e., the legislator); (2) some party being represented (i.e., the legislator's constituents); (3) something that is being represented (i.e., opinions, preferences, interests, identity, etc.); and (4) a setting within which the activity of representation is taking place (i.e., the legislature). While the role of the representative to "re-present" the views, beliefs, and political preferences of their constituents in a legislative body may seem relatively straightforward, in practice, representation is a difficult ideal to realize. One of the biggest obstacles to ideal political representation is the **principal-agent problem**. The principal-agent problem arises when one person or persons (the agent) is tasked to make decisions on behalf of another person or persons (the principal). The dilemma stems from two essential characteristics of someone trying to act on behalf of the other: (1) the agent has motivations and preferences of his or her own and (2) the agent has more information than the principal. Thus the dynamic between the principal and agent is governed by asymmetric information, where the agent knows more than the principal about a given action to be taken on behalf of the principal. Given the principal's relative ignorance, it is hard for the principal to determine whether the agent's actions are really in favor of the principal or not. This makes it difficult for the principal to tether the agent to the principal's best interests and thus hold them accountable for bad outcomes. Furthermore, where the agent and principal have divergent preferences on what action should be taken on behalf of the principal, a conflict of interest can frustrate the relationship and defeat the representation ideal.

The principal-agent problem is certainly at play when a representative is faced with casting a vote on a bill in the legislature. But there is a threshold issue for political representatives that adds a layer of additional uncertainty. Since representatives represent geographic areas full of principals, a representative must first determine what the "interests" of the people he is representing are. This is much simpler when one is representing an individual or a small group of people. A constituency is large, diverse, and almost certainly includes persons with diametrically opposed interests, beliefs, and values. It is thus impossible for a representative to strictly represent the interests of all of his constituents. Rather, he must endeavor to act in ways that serve the majority of his constituents. But how does the representative determine what the majority of her constituents want? And does acting in the best interest of the constituents mean relying on indicators of constituent preferences, or should the representative make his or her own determination of what is in their best interest independent of constituent opinion? Should the representative merely conduct a poll of his or her constituents and vote accordingly, or should she follow the dictates of her own conscience and intellect? Here we can see the problem of asymmetric information: legislators often have more information about a bill and what it will do than their average constituent. Indeed, most members of the electorate pay little attention to politics and are largely uninformed and unconstrained in their political and policy preferences. Perhaps if they had better information, the poll results would be different. Consider the Texas budget. In the past session, the Texas state legislature passed a $564.6 million supplemental budget bill to fund budget authorizations and to pay for the health care plan for retired teachers. Should Representative Travis Clardy (House District 11) and Senator Robert Nichols (Senate District 3) vote for the bill? Should they poll their constituents and vote accordingly, or should they act on their constituent's behalf in their best interests as the representatives see fit? Do you think their constituents know enough about the bill and the related issues to form an opinion on the vote? This question is at the heart of the dichotomy of representational roles: the delegate versus the trustee.

The trustee and delegate **models of representation** provide roadmaps for legislators that lead them in two widely divergent directions. In 1774, the great political thinker and member of the British parliament, Edmund Burke, gave voice to the trustee model of representation in his "Speech to the Electors of Bristol." In it, Burke argued that representatives must put the interests of the nation before both their personal interests and that of their constituents. Thus Burke advocated representatives should ignore "mandates" from their constituents and instead pursue the goal of protecting and serving the nation. Burke emphasized the asymmetric information advantage the representative has over his constituents. He argued that members of the legislature should follow their own assessment rather than that of constituents, who would tend to form their opinions narrowly and superficially. In contrast, we have the model of representation widely adopted by the delegates to the Second Continental Congress in issuing the Declaration of Independence: the delegate model. There, a representative was to serve as an organ of the constituent legislative assemblies. Indeed, the New York delegates abstained from the final vote on the Declaration of Independence because they lacked new instructions from the state legislature in New York. James Madison is one of the leading political thinkers and American Founders, and he advocated the delegate model of representation. For Madison and like-minded political philosophers, the delegate model requires the representative to serve as the mouthpiece of their constituents, and their own views on what is best or what should be done should be excluded from their voting decisions. The prevailing view was that it was the representatives' duty to obey the instructions of his or her constituents.

A third, "Goldilocks" type of representation has been identified by political theorists, recognizing that in practice representatives rarely follow either the delegate or trustee model exclusively. The politico model of representation is a hybrid of the delegate and trustee models that is intended to more closely reflect how representatives actually behave in office. The politico model recognizes that not all issues that a legislature grapples with are equal, that representatives regularly weigh input from a number of competing interests, and that public opinion plays a role in the decision-making process. A representative following the politico model as a guide uses his own personal judgment on issues with low salience among their constituents, while on salient political issues the politico tends to follow the opinion of their constituents. Generally, a politico mixes the two strategies and favors one or the other consideration depending on how important the issue to his constituents and how relevant the representative personally believes public opinion is to the issue at hand.

These models of representation focus on the role of the legislator (agent) to the constituent (principal) in terms of delivering substantive policy in the form of votes on legislation. However, this is only one kind of representational outcome. The delegate/politico/trustee models of representation all focus on substantive representation (i.e., actions taken on behalf of or in the interest of the represented as a substitute for their own actions). In the legislative context, substantive representation would include passing laws, oversight of agencies, and authorizing budgets for administrative agencies. Many would argue this is the essence of representation—serving the ends of constituents through the delivery of policy outcomes. However, there is another, perhaps equally important, facet of representation: descriptive representation. The idea of descriptive representation is that it is important that representatives reflect the race, language, class, income, gender, and/or occupational characteristics of the population that the given political institution is set to represent. How important is it that your agents in the legislature, the representatives who are tasked with the responsibility of acting on your behalf at the seat of government, look, act, and have a similar background and shared heritage as yourself? Another important American political thinker and Founder of the American Republic, John Adams, emphasized the importance of descriptive representation in the legislature. John Adams wrote that a representative assembly "should be in miniature an exact portrait of the people at large. It should think, feel, reason, and act like them." This is more commonly known as **microcosm theory**: the idea that a representative institution should be a microcosm of the greater population in reflecting its important demographic and cultural characteristics.

Assessing the Texas Legislature in Terms of Descriptive and Substantive Representation

Whether you favor substantive over descriptive representation, both aspects of representation are clearly important in nurturing and facilitating democratic representation. Consider the comparison of the demographics of the 84th Texas Legislature to the 2015 Texas population as depicted in Table 1.2. Setting aside the question of whether the Texas state legislature does an adequate job of substantive representation of the Texas citizenry, is the current Texas Legislature descriptively representative of the average Texas citizen? In terms of gender and race, it is clear that the Texas Legislature is not descriptively representative of the general Texas population. While the breakdown on gender in Texas is roughly 50/50, nearly 80% of the representatives to the Texas legislature are male. Whites are overrepresented in the Texas legislature by a full twenty percentage points, while all other racial/ethnic categories are underrepresented in the 84th Texas Legislature. The Texas Legislature skews older than the general Texas population, particularly in the higher and lower age categories. While twenty-one-year-olds qualify to serve in the Texas State House per the Texas Constitution, very few representatives in the Texas Legislature (6.2%) are thirty-five years old or younger. And there are twice as many 55–64-year-olds in the Texas Legislature as there are in the Texas population. The biggest disparity between the Texas Legislature and the Texas citizenry, however, is in education. Close to 70% of the Texas citizenry have a high school degree or less, while less than 2% of the Texas Legislature falls in that category. Just as stark is the difference between the percentage of the Texas Legislature with post-graduate work (51.1%) and that of the Texas population (8.3%). When we contrast the fact that over 90% of the representatives to the Texas legislature have a bachelors' degree or better with the fact that only 25% of the Texas citizenry do, it is more than apparent that education is the characteristic where the Texas Legislature is least consistent with microcosm theory. Nearly all of the representatives to the Texas State Houses are drawn from the educational elite in the state.

TABLE 1.2   How Representative is the Texas Legislature?

Demographics	84th Texas Legislature (2015)		2015 Texas Population
	Number	**Percentage**	**Percentage**
SEX			
Male	142	79.8%	49.6%
Female	36	20.2%	50.4%
AGE			
21–35 years old	11	06.2%	23.8%
35–44 years old	44	24.7%	14.8%
45–54 years old	45	25.3%	14.1%
55–64 years old	48	27.0%	12.3%
65+ years old	30	16.9%	11.2%
RACE/ETHNIC			
White	115	64.6%	44.0%
Hispanic	41	23.0%	38.4%
African American	19	10.7%	12.4%
Asian American	3	01.7%	03.4%
EDUCATION			
High School or Less	2	01.1%	68.4%
Some College	9	05.1%	06.3%
Bachelor's Degree	76	42.7%	17.1%
Post-Graduate Study	91	51.1%	08.3%
INCOME	Salary + *per diem*		Median Household Income
Average Income	$28,200		$51,900

Thus, it's fair to say that the Texas Legislature, in important ways, fails to conform to the expectations of microcosm theory. But it is also fair to ask whether Adams' theory about the proper characteristics of a representative assembly should be the goal. How important is it that the legislature looks like the citizenry? For example, we could certainly argue that it is good the Texas Legislature skews toward older (i.e., more experienced) and more educated representatives than does the general population. Certainly older, better educated representatives would be better situated to serve as trustees. Depending on which substantive representation model (delegate vs. trustee) we adopt, descriptive representation may be an irrelevant, even contradictory, goal.

As noted in the previous section, one significant difference between the US Congress and the Texas state legislature is the size of their respective upper and lower houses. As illustrated in Table 1.1, both the US House of Representatives (435) and Senate (100) have approximately three times as many members as the Texas State House (150) and State Senate (31). The fact that the US Congress is larger than the Texas state legislature isn't surprising at first blush, given the substantial difference in the population and geographic areas the respective legislative institutions represent. However, the size of the legislature with respect to the population it represents is a significant structural component of political representation (formalistic representation). The larger and more diverse the constituency of each individual member of the legislature, the more difficult it is for the legislature to be descriptively representative and comport with microcosm theory. Also, it exacerbates the principal-agent problem and complicates delegate model representation, as a heterogeneous district's constituent preferences are harder to divide, even in the modern age of scientific polling. Yet, increasing the number of representatives in a legislature is not a costless exercise. Legislatures must also be effective lawmaking institutions. The more members, the more difficult it is to organize the policy process, structure debate and discussion of legislation, and paradoxically, the greater need for a strong hierarchy to offset the unwieldiness of the larger body.

Figure 1.1 depicts the fifty state legislatures in terms of the absolute number of representatives in the legislature and the ratio of the seats in the legislature to the state population. New Hampshire's legislature stands out as the largest state legislature, with well over 400 members. And since New Hampshire is a small state in population terms relative to the other states in the Union, it is a substantial statistical outlier in its ratio of seats to the state population. California, on the other hand, if compared to other state legislatures' absolute number of seats, is near the middle of the pack. However, when we take into account the ratio of seats to the population, California representatives have the largest state constituencies for each member of their legislature. The Texas Constitution sets the Texas Senate at thirty-one seats and ninety-three as the minimum number of seats for the Texas State House. Texas has the eleventh largest legislature of the fifty states in terms of the absolute number of seats, but has the second largest state-population-to-seat ratio. So while the Texas Legislature is a fairly large state legislature in absolute terms, compared to the legislatures of the fifty states, Texas's large population relative to the number of seats in the legislature results in the second largest state House and Senate districts in the country. This raises legitimate concerns about the descriptive representation of the Texas state legislature and perhaps at least partially explains the descriptive demographic disparities depicted in Table 1.2. Larger districts are more likely to be heterogeneous. That

Figure 1.1   ■   Absolute and Relative Size of State Legislatures—Total Seats vs. Ratio of Seats to Population

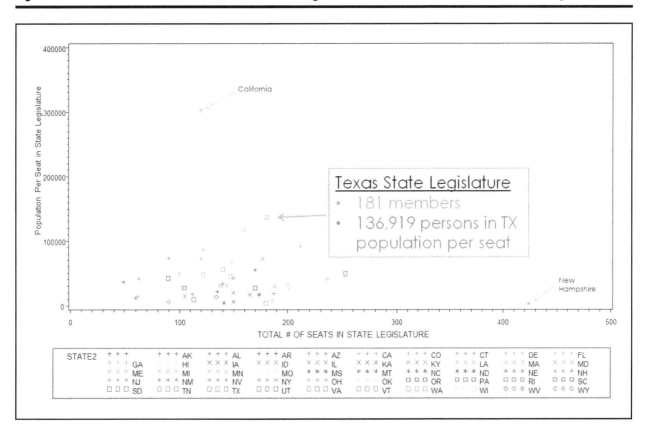

said, a constitutional change to increase the size of the Texas state legislature might make it a less effective policy-making and substantively representative assembly. This demonstrates the trade-off between legislative efficiency and substantive effectiveness versus descriptive representation in determining the size of a legislative body.

While larger districts may theoretically be more heterogeneous, the modern trend in representative districts has been toward greater homogeneity. The Big Sort over the past four decades has resulted in more lopsided representative districts in terms of their partisan preferences. Texas has been no exception. Consistent with the delegate model of representation, representatives to the Texas Legislature, like their constituents, have become more partisan and more ideologically polarized. Political polarization is the phenomenon where an ideological gap widens between groups of individual voters or between the constituencies of geographic political units. Increasing political polarization was likely a factor in the partisan battle over the 2003 redistricting bill in the Texas Legislature discussed at the beginning of the chapter. The impact of political polarization on substantive representation in the Texas state legislature can be seen in Figure 1.2. It shows the ideological estimates (based on votes in regular and special sessions) for the 2010 State Senate and the 2014 State House of the Texas state legislature. In both institutions, the ideological polarization that has emerged between the Republican and Democratic representatives is evident. Whereas in the past the political parties were fairly heterogeneous—particularly in the South where political conservatives regularly found a home in the Democratic Party—today, both the national and state political parties and their respective legislators are increasingly ideologically polarized between the parties and ideo-

FIGURE 1.2   ■   Legislator Ideological Estimates by Political Party for 2014 Texas State House and 2010 Senate

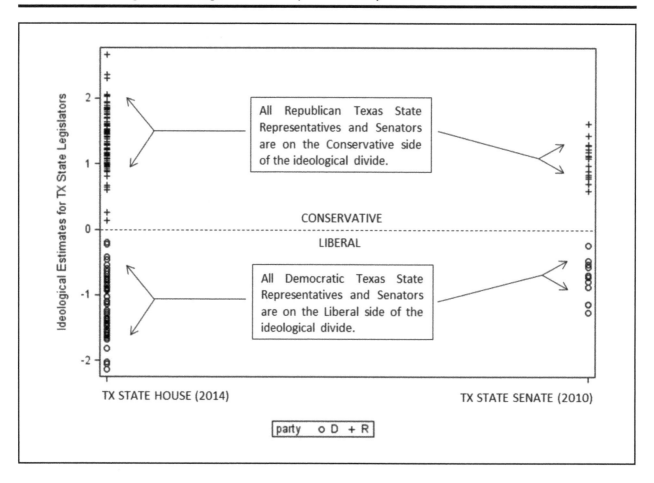

logically homogenous within the parties. In Figure 1.2, we see that there are no Democratic representatives or senators who fall on the conservative side of the ideological divide, nor are there any Republican representatives or senators who are liberal ideologically. Additionally, we see evidence of the national impact of political polarization, as Texas, a "Red" state in the modern era, reflects an overall rightward shift toward ideological conservatism. The Republicans in the Texas State House and Senate are more conservative than the Democrats in the Texas Legislature are liberal. Thus Texas is increasingly represented by conservative Republicans, and those Republicans are more conservative than the Democrats in the state are liberal. Political polarization clearly has a significant and important influence on substantive representation in the Texas state legislature. Given the overall trends, we can expect this factor to increase in the legislative terms to come. We should expect policy from the Texas state legislature to increasingly conform to the agenda of conservatives.

Goldilocks "Just Right" or Bearishly Too Cold? Where Texas Fits in the State Legislature Trichotomy

Traditionally, state legislatures have been characterized as part-time citizen legislatures versus the full-time professional legislatures of national governments. A citizen legislature is defined as a lawmaking assembly where the representatives are amateur citizens who have full-time occupations outside of the legislature and where the legislature provides sparse and limited resources and compensation to legislators. A professional legislature is a lawmaking assembly where the representatives are full-time legislators and are compensated accordingly. Professional legislatures provide legislators with substantial resources in terms of staff and office budgets. However, more recent scholarship has pointed to the fact that the diversity in institutional design for representative assemblies across the states produces shades of gray between citizen and professional legislatures. Consequently, a third, middle category has been created to account for legislatures that combine aspects of professional and citizen legislatures: the hybrid legislature. Table 1.3 outlines the **trichotomy of state legislatures**: citizen, hybrid, and professional and distinguishes between them on the basis of their differing purposes, meeting frequency, compensation, and staff and resources.

The purpose of a citizen legislature is to limit the power of the government by restricting the time and resources the lawmaking body can put in to lawmaking, and by discouraging careerism in the legislature by having part-time, amateur legislators. The theory being that intrusive lawmaking and

TABLE 1.3 Typologies of State Legislatures			
Characteristics	**Citizen Legislature**	**Hybrid Legislature**	**Professional Legislature**
Purpose	Limit role of state legislator to part-time function so that most citizens can serve.	To combine some of the limitations of the CL model with some of the benefits of professionalization in the PL model.	Professionalized legislators to deal with the size, scope, and complexity of legislative issues in the modern era.
Meetings	Biennial	Biennial or Annual	Annual
Compensation	Low	Medium	High
Time in Session	Low	Medium	High
Staffs	Small	Medium	Large
Resources	Low	Medium	High

corruption would be constrained where legislators served in temporary posts and consequently lacked the capacity to aggrandize power and sequester resources. The Founders of the United States strongly favored citizen legislatures for precisely this reason, and it is one of the primary motivations for Adam's microcosm theory and Madison's advocacy of the delegate model of representation. On the other hand, professional legislatures are designed to "level up" the institutional capacity of the legislature so that it can deal with an increasingly complex and interconnected political and social environment. Advocates for professional legislatures, such as Nelson Polsby, argue that well-bounded and thus professional legislatures are necessary to develop the internally complex, universalistic institutional rules essential to developing legislative policy expertise and experience. Hybrid legislatures try to have their cake and eat it too by combining some of the characteristics of citizen legislatures to capitalize on the descriptive representation and limited government benefits of that design, while providing sufficient resources and compensation to enable the legislature to pass effective legislation and regulation required in a sophisticated political economy. While the intent is clearly to achieve a "just right" Goldilocks outcome through a blend of the legislative archetypes, hybrid legislatures tend to lean strongly in one direction or the other.

The Texas Legislature falls within the hybrid legislature category. According to the National Conference of State Legislatures, Texas falls in the middle of state legislatures in terms of average job time, compensation, and total staff. However, a number of the characteristics of the Texas Legislature hearken back to the citizen legislatures of old. Texas is one of eight states in the Union that continues to have a biennial term—the legislature meets every other year rather than annually as most legislatures do. Furthermore, the compensation for legislators skews toward the citizen legislature level (approximately $19,000). The actual salary for Texas legislators, $7,200 a year, is actually low even for citizen legislatures. However, when you take into account benefits such as the *per diem* provided to offset expenses during the legislative session, the actual compensation is approximately $28,200 in an odd-numbered year and $35,400 for a two-year term, as specified in Table 1.2. While higher than the average compensation for citizen legislatures, it is far below the average compensation for hybrid legislatures (approximately $43,000). As those who favor citizen legislatures see it, the low compensation for representatives and short in-session time frames are a feature, not a bug. These features are designed to discourage careerism and the pursuit of enrichment through political relationships. Staff size in the Texas Legislature, on the other hand, is consistent with that of professional legislatures. Texas has the third largest combined permanent and session staff size in the country (2,388), trailing only Pennsylvania and New York. It is far in excess of the average staff size for professional legislatures (1,340), according to the NCSL. This feature is designed to provide sufficient resources to legislators for research and bill-writing. Given the size and diversity of the Texas economy, this component of professional legislatures is essential for the effective functioning of the Texas Legislature in developing state-wide public policy.

The Electoral Connection in the Texas Legislature

The basic qualifications for serving in the Texas state legislature are defined by the Texas Constitution and outlined in Table 1.1. In order to serve in the Texas House, a person must have lived in their district for at least one year, been a Texas resident for at least two years, and be at least twenty-one years old. In order to serve in the Texas Senate, you must have been a resident of Texas for five years, lived in the district for a year, and be at least twenty-six years old. Given the geographic size and strength of the economy in Texas, it should come as no surprise that Texas state legislative elections are fairly expensive. In the 2009–2010 electoral cycle, the average Texas State House race cost $274,734, while the average Texas Senate race cost $317,550. Texas has the second most expensive state house legislative campaigns, trailing only California, and the sixth most expensive state Senate legislative campaigns (after Illinois, California, Alabama, New York, and Missouri).

Per the Texas Constitution, elections for the Texas State House and the Texas State Senate are held in **single member districts**: only one person is elected to represent the district in the legislature. Thus elections to the Texas state legislature are winner-take-all elections, as there is only one seat per district, per election. In most electoral cycles there are two elections: the primary election and the general election. The primary election is to determine what candidate will represent a particular political party in the general election. So Republican candidates will square off in a Republican primary for a state legislative seat to determine who will be the Republican nominee in the general election for that seat. Likewise for the Democrats, Libertarians, and other political parties seeking to contest that election. The general election is the election that determines what candidate will win the seat and represent the district in the state legislature.

This chapter began with a story about a political battle in the Texas state legislature over redistricting. Texas has had many political battles over redistricting. Redistricting is the process of drawing electoral districts: the geographic territories from which political office holders are elected. In the case of the state legislature, the state is divided into districts equivalent to the number of seats in the respective houses. Thus there are currently thirty-one state Senate districts and ninety-three state House districts. Districts must be whole and contiguous: district lines must border one another and a district's lines must encapsulate a singular area constituting the whole of the district. Redistricting is the process of redrawing those lines. Per Article 3, § 28, The Texas Constitution entrusts the authority to draw and redraw district lines to the Texas state legislature or, should the legislature fail to pass a constitutional redistricting plan, the Texas Redistricting Board. As we noted in the 2003 redistricting controversy, gerrymandering is redistricting for political purposes. There are two types of gerrymandering: packing and diffusion. A packing gerrymander is an effort to locate an opposing party's voters all into one district or just a few districts, thus making that party uncompetitive in the majority of districts in the state. Whereas a diffusion gerrymander is designed to spread the opposing party's voters among multiple districts such that that it is difficult for them to win a plurality in any one district. Both strategies are designed to win more seats for the party controlling the redistricting process than they might otherwise win if the lines were neutrally drawn. The Supreme Court has ruled that partisan gerrymandering is constitutional, and it upheld the controversial gerrymandering at issue in the 2003 controversy.

Texas Legislative Organization: Committees

The Texas Legislature is organized into committees: sub-groups of the legislature organized with a specific or general mandate for legislative action. Nelson Polsby identified committees as the hallmark of legislative institutionalization. Committees allow for a greater volume of legislative output and a more efficient commitment of resources and expertise to the legislative process. Committees also promote access for citizens and organized interests to the legislative process. Committees signal to interested parties that they are considering bills that are important to those interests and related to their areas of focus and specialization. Committees serve an important informational function in the legislative process, allowing for members to develop expertise in issue areas and thus better write laws and regulations to be enacted. Committees are defined by two primary characteristics: jurisdiction and duration. Jurisdiction refers to the defined issue and policy areas in which the committee exercises primary authority to consider bills. Duration has to do with whether the committee is permanent or temporary. Permanent committees have unlimited duration, they exist from term to term subject only to a change to the institutional structure of the legislature (sometimes permanent committees are eliminated or combined). Temporary committees have a defined and limited duration, where the committee only exists for a specific task or for a specific time. There are a number of types of committees in the Texas Legislature. There are (1) standing committees, (2) subcommittees, (3) joint committees, (4) conference committees, and (5) interim committees. **Standing committees** are permanent committees, meaning they have an indefinite duration, and they have defined jurisdictions over specific political issues and subject areas. For example, the House Committee on County Affairs is a standing committee that "stands" from term to term (unless altered or eliminated by the House) and has jurisdiction over bills and policy related to county and municipal government in the state of Texas. A list of the standing committees for the Texas State House and Senate is reported in Table 1.4. Note that the Texas Senate has fewer committees, a function of the fact that the Texas Senate is a smaller body than the Texas House. Committees in the Texas Legislature are defined by their primary subject-matter jurisdictions. Thus the Texas House Energy Resources committee deals with

TABLE 1.4 Standing Committees in the 84th Texas Legislature		
Texas House of Representatives		**Texas Senate**
Agriculture & Livestock	International Trade & Intergovernmental Affairs	Administration
Appropriations	Investments & Financial Services	Agriculture, Water & Rural Affairs
Business & Industry	Judiciary & Civil Jurisprudence	Business & Commerce
Calendars	Juvenile Justice & Family Issues	Criminal Justice
Corrections	Land & Resource Management	Education
County Affairs	Licensing & Administrative Procedures	Finance
Criminal Jurisprudence	Local & Consent Calendars	Health & Human Services
Culture, Recreation, & Tourism	Natural Resources	Higher Education
Defense & Veterans' Affairs	Pensions	Intergovernmental Relations
Economic & Small Business Development	Public Education	Natural Resources & Economic Development
Elections	Public Health	Nominations
Energy Resources	Redistricting	State Affairs
Environmental Regulation	Rules & Resolutions	Transportation
General Investigating & Ethics	Special Purpose Districts	Veteran Affairs & Military Installations
Government Transparency & Operation	State Affairs	
Higher Education	Transportation	
Homeland Security & Public Safety	Urban Affairs	
House Administration	Ways & Means	
Human Services	Emerging Issues In Texas Law Enforcement, Select	
Insurance	State & Federal Power & Responsibility, Select	

legislation on issues like oil and gas exploration and wind farming, while the Senate Education committee considers legislation that includes setting educational standards for Texas primary and secondary schools and authorizing funding for the universities and colleges in the various Texas higher education systems.

Committees have two primary legislative venues: **mark-up sessions** and public hearings. Committees hold public hearings in order to get public reaction to proposed legislation as well as hear from experts and interested, involved parties and stakeholders who provide the committee with scientific studies as well as lay and expert testimony on the potential policy impact of a proposed bill. The mark-up session is where the committee considers each part of a proposed bill and votes on the language of specific provisions on the bill. Members of the Texas House of Representatives sit on at least one committee, and sometimes several. They are assigned to committees based on seniority and at the discretion of the Speaker of the House. Senators generally sit on a number of committees. The lieutenant governor assigns senators to committees. Committees are required to conduct business in open meetings.

While in the US Congress all standing committees are chaired by the majority party, which assigns a numerical majority of its members to each committee; this is not the case in the Texas Legislature. Texas has a long tradition of bipartisanship in the Texas Legislature, though that tradition has been challenged by political polarization in Texas politics. Nonetheless, the tradition of the minority party having majority membership and chair positions on some committees in the Texas legislature continues to this day. The House Committee on County Affairs was chaired by Rep. Garnet Coleman, a Democrat representing downtown Houston, in the 84th session of the Texas state legislature, despite the fact that the Republicans are the majority party in the Texas State House. Committees in the Texas Legislature may be further subdivided into subcommittees, a subset of the full committee that has jurisdiction over certain specific political issues within the general subject-area jurisdiction of the full committee. Subcommittees are considered by legislative scholars to be the "workhorse" of the national legislature, as the actual work writing and revising bills tends to happen at the subcommittee level there. Most committees in the Texas legislature are not subdivided into subcommittees, but those that are also use them as workhorses on legislation. For example, the Texas House Appropriations Committee, the committee responsible for creating spending bills, has seven subcommittees responsible for such specific government spending as Business & Economic Development, Criminal Justice, Education, Health and Human Services, and there is even the Hurricane subcommittee. A bill is first assigned to a committee and then sent to a subcommittee by the committee chair. The subcommittee reports to the committee, and the committee then reports to the full chamber. Before reporting to the chamber, a fiscal note or impact statement regarding the bill may be required that provides information about the impact of the bill on state agencies. This is created by the Legislative Budget Board and is important as it may affect the final vote on the bill.

House Concurrent Resolution 56 and Senate Concurrent Resolution 9 adopted during the regular session of the 84th legislature, authorizes the lieutenant governor and the Speaker of the House of Representatives for the Texas Legislature to create joint committees to study issues of special legislative concern upon mutual agreement. These committees are constituted by members of both the Texas State House and the Texas State Senate. Joint committees are temporary committees, meaning they have a defined and limited duration, that handle special topics—specific issues rather than general subject-area jurisdiction. For example, the 84th legislature created a joint committee to review the Texas Lottery and charitable bingo in Texas.

The Texas Constitution requires that in order for a bill to go to the governor's desk, it must have been passed in the same form by both the House and the Senate. Conference committees consist of five members from each chamber and are formed to reconcile the two different version of a bill passed on the Senate and the House, if such differences exist. The members from the House and the

Senate must reach a consensus on a compromise version of the legislation developed from the different chambers' versions of a bill. This kind of bill is reported out in a conference report that contains a **reconciliation bill**, the compromise bill between the House and Senate versions. **Interim committees** are committees that are brought together in-between the legislative session to handle important issues. For example, introduced in the 84th session the Texas Legislature was a bill providing for an interim study to examine what health and human services programs currently run by the state could be privatized. Unlike the other types of committees, there is no analog in the US Congress for interim committees, as the US Congress meets annually and not biennially.

A committee's activity can result in a number of different legislative outputs beyond legislative bills (laws). For example, joint committees are tasked with issuing reports on the study of a particular issue which may be the subject of future legislation. Sometimes the committee chooses not to report on a bill, essentially killing it in the committee. The committee may recommend amendments or even introduce a new version of the bill. Also, the committee may recommend where the bill shall be placed on the calendar—the **legislative calendar** is a schedule for consideration of bills. A legislature can have multiple calendars, depending on the type of legislative activity being scheduled. Next we will consider the specific process in the Texas Legislature whereby a bill becomes a law.

How a Bill Becomes a Law in Texas

The lawmaking process in the Texas state legislature is depicted in Figure 1.3, and it is closely modeled off of the legislative process for the US Congress. The first step in the process is for a Texas legislator to draft and introduce a bill or resolution. While we are familiar with bills, resolutions are a different kind of legislative output. **Resolutions** are less common than bills, and are used to handle specific activities of the legislature and are used most commonly to propose amendments to the Texas Constitution and for housekeeping functions, such as the previously mentioned resolution to allow the creation of joint committees. Resolutions are also used to give direction to state agencies and officials or express opinions or sentiments of public interest. There are three types of resolutions: joint resolutions, concurrent resolutions, and simple resolutions. Joint resolutions are used to propose and ratify amendments to the Texas Constitution or call for a Constitutional Convention to amend the US Constitution. Concurrent resolutions are from both houses of the Texas Legislature and are used when both houses are involved with a particular matter, such as the procedures and operations of the Texas Legislature that impact both houses. Simple resolutions pertain to procedural matters of just one chamber of the Texas Legislature. Only concurrent resolutions, and only where the concurrent resolution does not pertain to matters solely between the two chambers, must be sent to the governor for his or her signature. Otherwise, resolutions cannot be vetoed by the governor.

Legislative bills are the exclusive legislative instrument to create laws and regulations and are the subject of most legislative activity. They are the only method to introduce, enact, and amend or repeal a law. Texas legislators sometimes draft bills on their own, but they may use the services provided by the Texas Legislature (i.e., the Texas Legislative Council). They may also rely on interest groups or state agencies for providing specific language to include in a proposed bill. Texas legislators may sometimes co-author bills with other Texas legislators. However, the Legislative Budget Board (LBB) must draft appropriations bills (bills that provide funds). As noted earlier in the chapter, the LBB consists of members of both chambers of the legislature, and is co-chaired by the Speaker of the House and the lieutenant governor. A bill may be introduced in either the Texas House or the Texas Senate. Each chamber has the right to amend, alter, and/or reject the bills of the other chamber.

FIGURE 1.3 ■ How a Bill Becomes a Law in the Texas Legislature*

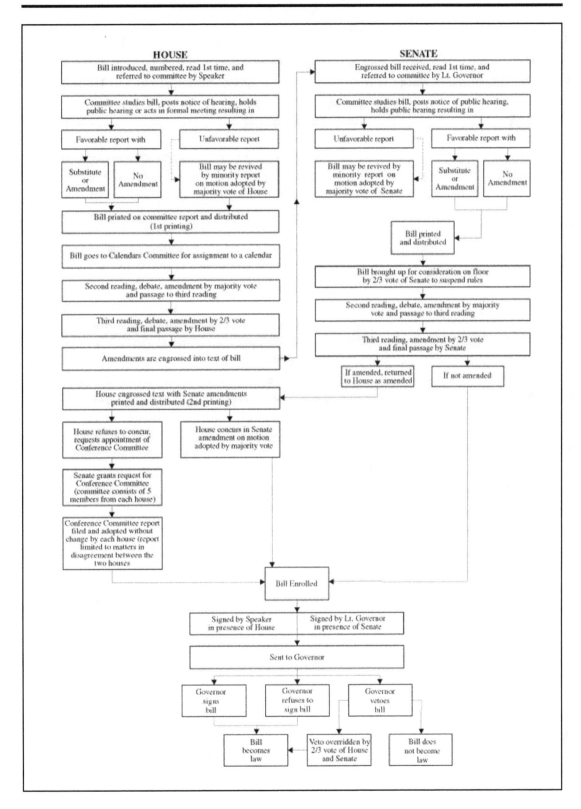

*This describes the legislative process for bills that originate in the House. The houses flip for bills that originate in the Senate.

The first step of the bill process is the introduction of a bill on the floor of one of the houses of the Texas Legislature. This is called the first reading of the bill. The bill is introduced on the floor, given a short description (caption), and assigned a number and subject. The Texas Constitution limits when bills may be introduced in a legislative session. Article 3, § 5 of the Texas Constitution creates a thirty-day window, starting from the first day of the session, that is exclusively for introducing bills in a legislative session. During that window, emergency matters and confirming appointments of the governor may also be introduced. In the thirty-day window that follows, bills can still be introduced (for a total of sixty days for bill introduction) but the legislature also will hold committee hearings, and for the remainder of the legislative session, the legislature may take action on bills, resolutions, and emergency matters. While bills may be introduced after the first sixty days of the session, the Texas House and Texas Senate rules of procedure provide that such bills, excepting emergency bills, require a four-fifths vote by the introducing chamber. The Texas Constitution, Article 3, Section 33 provides that all bills that are meant to raise revenue must originate in the House of Representatives.

After a bill is drafted, introduced and read on the floor, the second step in the process is to assign the bill to a committee. As previously noted, the amount of work on bills is voluminous, and this is doubly so given the short legislative period and biennial term of the Texas Legislature. Given the complexity of modern legislation and the heavy workload, the committee structure that divides the legislative responsibility among committees with subject-matter jurisdiction is essential to getting laws passed, amended, or repealed. Thus committees help relieve the work placed on the chamber as a whole. As noted in the earlier section, committees not only revise bills and report them to the floor, but they also have the power to kill bills. This gives committees the powerful role of **gatekeeper** in the legislative process—the committee determines what bills do and do not proceed forward. Only bills that garner the support of a majority of the members of the committee will ever make it to the floor for general debate. Close to 90 percent of all bills introduced in a session die in committee. For example, the bill on creating a study on the privatization of the health and human services programs, H.B. 2966, died in the House Human Services Committee in the 84th session. In the Texas House of Representatives, the Speaker of the House assigns bills to committees based on the subject of the bill, where particular committees handle particular subjects. This is required by the Texas House Rules of Procedure. The Texas Senate Rules of Procedure do not contain the same rule; however the lieutenant governor often follows the pattern of sending bills to committees that pertain to the same/similar subject as the bill. Once all public hearings on the bill are completed and committee work on the bill in mark-up session is finished, the committee holds a vote on the bill. If the committee chooses to take action by reporting the bill to the floor, they will issue a committee report on the bill expressing the committee's recommendations (favorable or unfavorable) and provide the text and procedural history of the bill and its amendments to the chamber's members.

The third step in the process, if a bill makes it out of committee, is to place the bill on the calendar for consideration by the chamber. A legislative calendar identifies and schedules bills and resolutions for floor action in chambers of the legislature. While there are calendars in both the Texas House and Senate, they do differ in a few important respects. The Texas House of Representatives has two committees that set the calendar for the session: the Committee on Calendars and the Committee on Local and Consent Calendars. The Texas House rules permit four types of calendars: the Daily House Calendar; the Supplemental House Calendar; the Local, Consent, and Resolutions Calendar; and the Congratulatory and Memorial Calendar. The different calendars group bills together based on category, which determines the calendar the bill will be placed on, such as the emergency calendar (supplemental) or the constitutional amendments calendar (daily). The Texas Senate has two calendars, the Intent Calendar and the Local and Uncontested Calendar. The Intent Calendar is for bills that may generate controversy or apply to state or regional political issues, and these bills are placed in the order in which they come out of committee. No bill or resolution may be considered on its first day on the Intent Calendar, and a vote of two-thirds of the members present is required before any of the measures listed on the Intent Calendar may be debated. The Senate rules do not require measures to be brought up for consideration in the order listed on the Intent Calendar, and the Senate routinely considers only a portion of those measures listed on the Intent Calendar for a given day. A senator must give notice from day to day for a measure that was not brought up for consideration to remain on the Intent Calendar. Any provision of the Senate rule governing the Intent Calendar may be suspended by a vote of four-fifths of the members present. Both chambers provide for the consideration of local and noncontroversial bills separately from other business on the respective legislative calendars for the same. These are either bills that deal with only a particular town, city, or locality or where no opposition to the bill is anticipated.

The fourth step in the process is floor action—debate on and consideration of the bill on the floor of the chamber. The first floor consideration of a bill occurs on the second reading of the bill—the bill is read for the second time, by caption only, and is then subject to debate and amendment by the full membership of the chamber. Any member may offer an amendment to the bill; it is adopted subject to majority assent in a vote by the full chamber. Under Article 3, § 21 of the Texas Constitution, Texas Senators and Texas Representatives cannot be questioned about what they may have said while engaged in debate on the floor of the Texas House or Texas Senate. This gives senators and representatives the opportunity to discuss potentially controversial subjects while in a debate and provides them with free speech protections.

There are a number of parliamentary rules and procedural gambits that legislators can play to delay or kill legislation they disfavor. Some of these strategies can be played in both houses of the Texas Legislature, while others can only be used in either the Texas House or the Texas Senate. A common legislative strategy used by legislative minorities is to attach a rider, a provision added to a bill that has little connection with the subject matter of the bill, in an attempt to pass a provision that lacks majority support. The rider piggybacks on the bill with majority support and thus passes. In Texas, a controversial rule permits a **closed rider**, where the additional provision is not made public until after the chamber has voted on it (but before the conference committee). A converse strategy to that of including an unpopular provision to a popular bill in order to have both pass is to use a rider to make the whole bill unpalatable to a majority of the chamber, thus ensuring that both fail (i.e., the **killer amendment**). This kind of amendment, also known as a "poison pill" or "wrecking" amendment, involves using an amendment to significantly change a bill's intent or effect in order to kill a bill that would have otherwise passed. Usually it involves proposing a change that has majority support but, once added to the bill under consideration, causes the whole bill to lose majority support. **Chubbing** is a uniquely Texan form of delaying action used in the Texas House by the minority to waste time on the floor and close the window of opportunity for a bill under consideration that they opposed. The technique involves extending debate on bills set earlier on the calendar such that bills they disfavor scheduled later for calendar never come up for consideration, effectively killing those bills by running out the clock.

There are several minority legislative strategies available only in the Texas Senate. One such strategy that can only be used in the Senate is a **blocker bill**. A blocker bill is a bill placed at the beginning of the daily calendar, having been quickly passed through committee, where it remains the rest of the session. No other bill can be passed unless at least two-thirds of the senators agree to suspend the rules and skip over the blocker bill. This procedural rule empowers voting minorities, particularly on controversial and partisan bills under consideration. In the Texas Senate, members have the opportunity, under the Texas Senate Rules of Procedure, to tag a bill. This halts all debate on the bill for forty-eight hours and the "tag" is not debatable. Another legislative strategy to thwart support for a bill is to **filibuster**. A procedural difference in floor action between the Texas House and Texas Senate is that, like the US Senate, Texas senators have the power to filibuster a bill. This is where a Senator maintains "control of the floor," after being recognized by the presiding officer, during debate on a bill. This technique brings a halt to normal order and no other official legislative business may be conducted so long as the Senator can keep talking and thus maintain control of the floor. The filibuster serves as a mechanism to kill the bill. Unlike the rules for the filibuster in the US Senate, a Texas Senator using this tactic cannot yield to other Texas senators or points of order, and must keep their remarks and debate focused on the particular topic of the bill being filibustered. If a Senator fails to abide by these rules, the presiding officer may require the Texas Senator to end the filibuster, after having been warned that he or she was not in line with the Senate rules (See Senate Rule 4.03).

On June 25, 2013, Texas Senator Wendy Davis held an eleven-hour-long filibuster during a special session of the Texas Legislature to block Senate Bill 5, a measure to impose more restrictive abortion regulations, such as a ban on abortions after twenty weeks of pregnancy and a provision that requires abortion clinics to meet the same health and safety standards of surgical centers in hospitals. Three hours short of midnight, Lieutenant Governor David Dewhurst ruled that Davis had gone off topic and thus called for a vote on whether the filibuster could continue. Despite Republican efforts to end the filibuster and call the vote, Democrats were able to delay the proceedings through parliamentary inquiries until midnight, ending the special session and thus killing the bill. However, the victory was short-lived, as Governor Rick Perry called a second special session to revive consideration of the abortion restrictions bill. The bill was eventually passed by both the Texas House and Senate in the July 2013 second special session. While it helped boost Wendy Davis into the national political spotlight, the control of the governor's office allowed Republicans to nullify the effort to filibuster the bill. The US Supreme Court issued a temporary stay of the law, and it will consider the constitutionality of Senate Bill 5 in its next session. Debate is much more restricted in the Texas House. In the Texas House of Representatives, the Speaker of the House recognizes who will speak, and those individuals are limited to ten minutes unless otherwise agreed to by majority vote (see House Rule 5, §28). In addition, Texas representatives cannot speak more than twice on a bill unless approved by the Texas House, and they can only speak the second time after all other members wishing to speak on the bill have had an opportunity to do so (see House Rule 5, § 29).

The fifth step in the process, once debate has been completed, is the third reading of the bill, which is followed by the call for a vote on final passage. In either house, a bill may be passed on a voice vote or a recorded vote, but most controversial bills will be conducted using a recorded vote. Members of the Texas Legislature are required to disclose any personal or private interest they may have in a particular vote and, if they had said interest, are not supposed to partake in the vote on that bill (Texas Constitution, Article 3, § 22). Article 3, § 37 of the Texas Constitution provides that "no bill shall be considered, unless it has been first referred to a committee and reported thereon, and no bill shall be passed which has not been presented and referred to and reported from a committee at least three days before the final adjournment of the Legislature." However this rule can be suspended by a four-fifths vote of the chamber considering the bill on the floor, and the rule is routinely suspended in the Texas Senate allowing for an immediate third reading after the second reading is finished. The Texas House, on the other hand, rarely suspends this rule. A simple majority vote is required to pass the bill on the third reading. Once the bill is passed it is engrossed, generating an official copy of the bill incorporating all corrections and amendments for consideration in the opposite chamber.

The sixth step, depending on passage in the originating chamber, is to send the bill to the opposite chamber for consideration. If a bill or resolution is defeated in a session in either chamber, it cannot be reintroduced during that session. A Senate or House member would need to wait until the next legislative session, in two years, in order to introduce the bill anew. After the bill is sent to the other chamber, it is subject to the entire assignment, committee consideration, and floor action process in the coordinate chamber. If the bill is passed by the other chamber with exactly the same language (agreeing to all amendments made by the other house), then both the Speaker of the House and lieutenant governor must sign the bill before it is enrolled, where a final copy of the bill as passed by both houses is printed for consideration by the governor. However, if, as is more often the case, there are differences between the two versions of the bill as passed in each of the chambers, then a conference committee is called to reconcile the two different versions of the bill. If the conference committee cannot come to an agreement on a version of the bill acceptable to them, then the bill dies. As mentioned earlier, when they do agree, a conference report is made with a reconciliation bill. This report is voted up or down in both houses with a closed rule, meaning no amendments to the reconciliation bill are allowed. Only a yes or a no vote on final passage is permitted. If it passes both houses, it again goes to the presiding officers for their signature and enrollment.

If the presiding officers of the Texas Legislature sign the bill, the seventh step is to send the bill to the Texas governor. The Texas governor may sign or veto the bill. If the bill is vetoed, a two-thirds majority vote in each chamber can override the governor's veto. If the governor takes no action the bill becomes law. If a bill is sent to the governor within ten days of final adjournment, the governor has until twenty days after final adjournment to sign the bill, veto it, or allow it to become law without a signature. After a law is passed, it takes ninety days for the law to go into effect unless both chambers vote by a two-thirds vote to say otherwise.

The Texas Legislature in Perspective: The 84th Session

The 84th session of the Texas Legislature witnesses a new political era dawn as a new governor and lieutenant governor took office. In the 2014 elections the Republicans strengthened their grip on the State House and Senate, and as illustrated in Figure 1.2, that majority is more ideologically conservative and polarized from the more moderate, but still distinctly liberal, Democrats. While the Republican majority has become more conservative, Joe Straus (R, San Antonio) was able to stave off a challenge from his Right to remain Speaker of the House. That said, it is no surprise that the more significant legislation passed by the 84th session moved the policy status quo even further rightward in a number of policy areas including taxes, energy, guns, health care, transportation, and drug policy. Governor Abbot saw a number of his legislative priorities successfully enacted into law, including greater funding for transportation, pre-kindergarten legislation, and incentives for higher education.

Approximately 6,200 bills and joint resolutions were filed this session, and more than 1,300 bills were sent to Governor Greg Abbot for his signature. The governor vetoed forty-four bills that reached his desk, including two ethics bills Governor Abbot sought as part of his ethics legislative priority. The vetoes were issued over the "spousal loophole" dealing with disclosure of personal finances of married elected officials. The House and Senate were able to reconcile the two competing budget bills, HB 1 and SB 2, in a conference committee settlement. The bill, while calling for a 3.6 percent increase over the current budget, left $2.9 billion under the state constitutional spending cap. On taxes, the chambers clashed over whether to prioritize business tax cuts or property tax cuts. In conference they compromised on a total of $3.8 billion tax cuts, combining to both cut the marginal business tax rate and property taxes. On energy, in response to the city of Denton's decision to ban hydraulic franking, HB 40 was proposed and signed into law preempting local regulation of oil and gas operations in the state of Texas. In a joint resolution, SCR 13/HCR 57, the Texas Legislature urged the US Congress to end the ban on crude oil experts. The 84th session of the Texas Legislature included two major provisions expanding the right of Texans to carry guns. Senate Bill 11 allowing handguns in dorms, classrooms, and campus buildings in Texas colleges and universities was signed into law by Governor Greg Abbot. Universities and colleges will still be able to establish their own rules on where handguns are carried and how they are stored; furthermore, only concealed handgun license holders, who are twenty-one years or older, will be allowed to carry their guns on campus. Private colleges are exempt from the law. Also this session, the legislature passed, and the governor signed, legislation permitting "open carry" in the state of Texas. House Bill 910 permits concealed handgun license holders (CHLs) to openly carry their guns in a belt or shoulder holster while in public. Several pieces of health care legislation were introduced to continue and consolidate the Health and Human Services agencies in the constitutionally required sunset review of HHSC authorizing legislation. In the area of transportation, the Texas Legislature passed a constitutional amendment to be ratified by the citizens of Texas expanding funding for road and highway infrastructure, while headway in the Senate was made on a ban of red light cameras, with the Senate Transportation committee passing SB 714. And finally, a number of bills were introduced to de-criminalize marijuana ranging from medical marijuana to recreational marijuana. Governor Abbot vowed to veto any marijuana-related legislation reaching his desk; however, one such bill was passed and signed into law. SB 339, the "Compassionate Use Act" creates a DPS-regulated license for an entity to operate as a dispensing organization to cultivate and dispense low-THC cannabis for medical purposes.

Key Terms

gerrymandering
quorum
special session
principal-agent problem
models of representation
microcosm theory
trichotomy of state legislatures
single member districts
standing committees
mark-up sessions
interim committees
reconciliation bill
legislative calendar
resolutions
gatekeeper
killer amendment
chubbing
blocker bill
filibuster
closed rider

quorum:

gerrymandering: redistricting for partisan advantage

References

A.P. "Justices Back Most G.O.P. Changes to Texas Districts." *The New York Times*, June 28, 2006.

Texas State House. *An Act Relating to an Interim Study Regarding the Identification of Health and Human Services Programs That Can Be Privatized.* 84th, H.B. 2966.

Alonso, Sonia, John Keane, and Wolfgang Merkel. *The Future of Representative Democracy.* Cambridge, MA: Cambridge University Press, 2011.

Batheja, Aman. "Senate Approves $564.6 Million Supplemental Budget Bill." *The Texas Tribune*, May 26, 2015.

Benning, Tom. "Texas Senate Committee Approves Bill That Would Put a Stop to Red-Light Cameras." *The Dallas Morning News*, April 13, 2015.

Bishop, Bill. *The Big Sort: Why the Clustering of Like-Minded America Is Tearing Us Apart.* Boston, MA: Mariner Books, 2009.

Blumenthal, Ralph. "Texas G.O.P. Is Victorious in Remapping." *The New York Times*, January 7, 2004.

Burke, Edmund. "Representation: Edmund Burke, Speech to the Electors of Bristol." In *The Founders' Constitution*, edited by Philip B. Kurland and Ralph Lerner. Chicago, IL: University of Chicago, 1987.

Casey, Linda, Nadeanne Haftl, Kevin McNellis, Robin Parkinson, Peter Quist, and Denise Roth Barber. "An Overview of Campaign Finances, 2009-2010 Elections." www.followthemoney.org: National Institution on Money in State Politics, 2012.

Chammah, Maurice. "Texplainer: What Is the Blocker Bill?" *The Texas Tribune*, January 28, 2013.

Griffith, Elmer Cummings. *The Rise and Development of the Gerrymander.* New York, NY: Kessinger Publishing, LLC, 1907.

Jasinski, Laurie E. "Legislative Budget Board." *Handbook of Texas Online*, 2010.

———. "Texas Legislative Council." *Handbook of Texas Online*, 2010.

Krehbiel, Keith. "Legislative Organization." *The Journal of Economic Perspectives* 18, no. 1 (2004): 113–28.

Lavandera, Ed. "Texas House Paralyzed by Democratic Walkout." *CNN Online*, 2003.

League of United Latin American Citizens V. Perry, 548 United States Reports 399 (2005).

LRLT. "Congressional Redistricting 2001-2003." In *Legislative Reference Library of Texas.* Austin, TX, 2004.

Madison, James, Alexander Hamilton, and John Jay. *The Federalist Papers.* Edited by Isaac Kramnick Harmondsworth: Penguin, 1787.

Mansbridge, Jane. "Rethinking Representation." *American Political Science Review* 97, no. 4 (2003): 515–28.

Mauzy V. Legislative Redistricting Board, 471 South Western Reporter 570 (1971).

McConachie, Lauros G. *Congressional Committees.* New York, NY: Thomas Y. Crowell & Co., 1898.

NCSL. "Full and Part-Time Legislatures." *National Conference of State Legislators*, June 1st, 2014.

Polsby, Nelson. "The Institutionalization of the US House of Representatives." *American Political Science Review* 62, no. 1 (March, 1968 1968): 144–68.

Pressley, Cindy. "The Texas Legislature." In *Texas Politics 142 Workbook*, 2013.

Price, Bob. "It's Official: Texas Legislature Passes Open Carry." Breitbart.com, http://www.breitbart.com/texas/2015/05/29/its-official-texas-legislature-passes-open-carry/.

Rakove, Jack N. *Original Meanings: Politics and Ideas in the Making of the Constitution.* New York, NY: Vintage Books, 1997.

Ramshaw, Emily. "A Filibuster Creates an Overnight Celebrity." *The New York Times* (2011). Published electronically June 4, 2011. http://www.nytimes.com/2011/06/05/us/05ttdavis.html?_r=0.

Schwartz, Nancy Lou. *The Blue Guitar: Political Representation and Community.* Chicago, IL: University of Chicago, 1988.

Shaw V. Reno, 509 United States Reports 630 (1993).

Shor, Boris, and Nolan McCarty. "Aggregate State Legislator Shor-Mccarty Ideology Data, June 2015 Update." Harvard Dataverse, 2015.

Sivtek, Patrick. "Abbot Wields Veto Pen in Final Days of Decision Period." *The Texas Tribune*, June 20, 2015.

Smith, Morgan. "Campus Cary Bill Heads to Gov. Abbot." *The Texas Tribune*, May 31, 2015.

Smith, Morgan, and Becca Aaronson. "Abortion Bill Finally Passes Texas Legislature." *The Texas Tribune*, July 13, 2013.

Staff. "About the Legislative Process in Texas." Texas Legislative Council, http://www.tlc.state.tx.us/gtli/legproc/process.html.

———. "Committees of the 84th Legislature." Texas State Legislature, http://www.senate.state.tx.us/75r/senate/Commit.htm.

———. "House Committees." Texas House of Representatives, http://www.house.state.tx.us/committees/.

———. "How a Bill Becomes a Law." Texas House of Representatives, http://www.house.state.tx.us/about-us/bill/.

———. "Other Legislation--Resolutions." Texas Legislative Council, http://www.tlc.state.tx.us/gtli/legproc/otherleg.html.

Barnhart Dictionary of Etymology. H.W. Wilson Co., 1988.

Staff, History.com. "Congress Votes for Independence." (2009). http://www.history.com/this-day-in-history/congress-votes-for-independence.

TLC. "Guide to Texas Legislative Information (Revised)." (2015): 11. Published electronically March 2015. http://www.tlc.state.tx.us/pubslegref/gtli.pdf.

TSA. "Summary of the 84th Texas Legislative Session." Texas Star Alliance, http://www.texasstaralliance.com/summary-of-the-84th-texas-legislative-session/.

Villacorta, Natalie, and Jennifer Haberkorn. "Supreme Court Blocks Texas Abortion Law Ruling." *Politico*, June 29, 2015.

Villafranca, Armando. "Life in Exile—Texas Eleven Say Constituents Oppose Remap." *Houston Chronicle*, August 4, 2003.

Weber, Andrew. "Texplainer: What Is Chubbing?" *The Texas Tribune*, Feburary 2, 2011.

Weberg, Brian. "Size of State Legislative Staff." edited by NCSL. www.ncls.org: National Conference of State Legislatures, 2009.

Wilkerson, John D. "Killer" Amendments in Congress." *American Political Science Review* 93, no. 3 (September, 1999): 535–52.

Exercise 1.1 ■ Multiple Choice

1. How many members does the Texas Senate have?
   a. 31
   b. 100
   c. 150
   d. None of the above

2. For how many days does the Texas Legislature meet?
   a. 140
   b. 175
   c. 365
   d. None of the above

3. In a general election for the Texas Senate, what type of vote is required?
   a. Majority vote
   b. Plurality vote
   c. Primary vote
   d. Run-off vote

4. What type of legislative committee is permanent, has an indefinite duration, and subject-matter jurisdiction?
   a. Conference committee
   b. Joint committee
   c. Interim committee
   d. None of the above

5. The _____ was promulgated by John Adams and stated that a representative institution should reflect the characteristics of the population that it represents.
   a. delegation imperative
   b. principal-agent model
   c. microcosm theory
   d. none of the above

6. The principal-agent relationship is problematic because the agent has _____ information when compared to that possessed by the agent.
   a. symmetric
   b. asymmetric
   c. plenary
   d. none of the above

7. The _____ model of representation was popularized by Edmund Burke and requires a representative to put the interests of the nation, as he or she sees it, before the interests of his or her constituents.
   a. politico
   b. trustee
   c. delegate
   d. none of the above

8. Which of the below minority legislative strategies is <u>not</u> exclusively used by the Senate?
   a. Chubbing
   b. Filibuster
   c. Blocker bill
   d. None of the above

9. A _____ type of legislature is populated by mostly amateur citizens with full-time occupations outside of the legislature, provides low compensation to representatives, and where the legislature has sparse and limited resources for lawmaking.
   a. professional
   b. citizen
   c. hybrid
   d. none of the above

10. A bill has been _____ when a final copy of the bill that has passed both houses of the Texas Legislature is printed for consideration by the governor.
   a. engrossed
   b. enrolled
   c. embalmed
   d. none of the above

Exercise 1.2 ■ Research Exercise

Use the Texas Legislature Online resource for bills (http://www.capitol.state.tx.us/MnuLegislation. aspx) to find a bill from the 84th session of the Texas Legislature to answer the following questions. Your bill must be a bill that was reported to the floor of one of the chambers and received a third reading.

1. What is the bill number? Which house did the bill originate in?

2. What is the caption for the bill?

3. Who authored the bill?

4. Who sponsored the bill? (include up to three names)

5. What committee was the bill assigned to?

6. What action did the committee take on the bill?

7. Did the committee hold public hearings on the bill? If so, when?

8. Did the committee amend the bill? Describe at least one such amendment or alteration to the bill from the committee mark-up session.

9. What floor action did the chamber take on the bill?

10. Provide a summary of how to follow a bill on the Texas Legislature Online website.

Exercise 1.3 ■ Writing Exercise

In this chapter we discussed a number of theories and models of political representation, types of legislatures, and how the structure and rules of legislatures affect the quality and nature of representation. Select one of the models or theories of representation from the chapter and write an amendment to the Texas Constitution which designs the Texas Legislature consistent with that theory of representation. Include the size, structure, compensation, and resources you wish to provide as part of your design. Explain how your design of the Texas Legislature is consistent with and supportive of your chosen theory of representation. What are the strengths of your design? What are the weaknesses? Would Edmund Burke applaud your design? Why or why not? Would John Adams cheer your model legislature? Why or why not?

CHAPTER 2

The Texas Governor: Politically Strong, Constitutionally Weak

Dr. Kwame Badu Antwi-Boasiako

Dr. Richard J. Herzog

This chapter discusses the elected governor in Texas. The governorship is politically strong but constitutionally weak. Despite the constitutional weaknesses associated with the office, a charismatic governor can enhance the limited executive, legislative, and judicial powers through both formal and informal roles of the office.[1] However, the governor is usually swamped with many tasks and bears the blame when things are not done right in Texas. It often becomes difficult for the governor to maintain a high approval rating while in office. In 2012, Governor Rick Perry, the longest serving governor in Texas history (2001–2015), struggled in the public opinion polls as the number of Texans that disapproved of his job performance was equal or greater than those that approved of his work. One reason, among others, for low approval ratings is that Texans generally distrust executive authority. In addition, Governor Perry's failed presidential campaign in 2012 did not enhance his stature in the Lone Star State.

With the election of many other top executives, including the lieutenant governor, attorney general, comptroller, agriculture commissioner, and land commissioner, Texas has a **plural executive** (see Chapter 3, The Texas Bureaucracy), which makes the governor constitutionally weak. Plural executive means other executive functions are divided to the various elected officials limiting the power of the governor. However, the governor does appoint people to several other state positions including, but not limited to, the Secretary of State, the Adjutant General, the Director of the Office of Community Affairs, and the Director of the Office of State-Federal Relations. Before the argument that the governor is constitutionally weak and politically strong is forwarded, some background information covering the governor and the plural executive will be helpful.

---

1. Ernest Crain and James Perkins. *Introduction to Texas Politics, 3rd ed.* (Wadsworth, Thomson Learning, 2000), 105.

Selection Process

In Texas, the governor is selected in a statewide election held during even-numbered years or **off years** when the country is not holding a presidential election. Many political scientists believe that keeping state and national politics separate are a good idea. If presidential and gubernatorial elections were held together, in the same year, it may appear that a president and governor are running together on the same political party ticket and voters are more likely to focus on national over state politics.

A Texas governor will be elected in November 2018, 2020, and 2024. Texas is a two-party state where gubernatorial candidates seek the endorsement of either the Democratic or Republican Party. Candidates for each party are chosen via primaries earlier in an election year. Independent candidates[2] must collect a required number of signatures in order to compete in the November general gubernatorial election. Usually, the contests for the governor's seat hardly focus on issues, but rather on personalities. Unlike the national presidential elections where the presidential candidates select a running mate, the would-be governor runs alone.

Terms and Tenure

Along with fourteen other states in the Union, Texas does not limit a governor's number of terms in office. A 1972 constitutional amendment went into effect in 1974 where the previous two-year term was extended to a **four-year term**. "Until World War II, Texas governors were routinely elected for two terms. During and after the War the precedent was supplanted by a trend to three terms."[3] Table 2.1 shows the most recent Texas governors. If a governor does not complete a term in office due to resignation, death, or impeachment, the lieutenant governor becomes governor. After Governor George W. Bush was declared the winner of the 2000 presidential election he vacated his position and the Lieutenant Governor, Rick Perry, then became the governor and served the remaining two years of Governor Bush's term. In the 2002 race for governor, the Republican Rick Perry defeated Tony Sanchez, the Democrat, by a vote of 2,632,591 (58%) to 1,819,798 (40%).[4] In 2006, Rick Perry won with 39% of the votes (1,716,792).[5] In 2010, Governor Perry defeated former Houston Mayor

TABLE 2.1 Texas Governors 1987–Present			
Governor	**Party**	**Term**	**Age***
Bill Clements	Republican	1987–1991	69
Ann Richards	Democrat	1991–1995	57
George W. Bush	Republican	1995–2001	48
Rick Perry	Republican	2001–2015	45
Greg Abbott	Republican	2015–present	57
*Age when taking oath of office.			

2. These are individuals who may be interested in the governorship but do not align or campaign on the platforms of either the Republican or Democratic Party. In addition those candidates do not go through primaries.

3. Richard H. Kraemer, Charldean Newell, and David F. Prindle, *Texas Politics, 7th ed.* (Wadsworth Publishing Company: Wadsworth, CA, 1999).

4. Texas Secretary of State at www.sos.state.tx.us/historical/index.shtml, accessed December 4, 2005.

5. Texas Secretary of State at http://elections.sos.state.tx.us/elchist.exe, accessed July, 25, 2008.

Mark White by a vote of 2,737,481 (54.97%) to 2,106,395 (42.29%).[6] In 2014 Governor Perry did not seek re-election, but did again seek the US presidency in 2016. In the November 2014 election the Republican candidate, Greg Abbott, defeated Wendy R. Davis, the Democratic Party candidate, by a vote of 2,796,274 (59.15%) to 1,835,896 (38.83%).[7]

Requirements for Office

In Texas, contrary to the US Constitution, the governor elect had to swear he or she had never fought in a duel, intended to fight in one, and acknowledged the existence of a Supreme Being[8] (See Texas Constitution Article 1, Section 4). Fortunately, the state has long laid those requirements to rest and the current requirements to pursue the governorship are thirty years of age, US citizenship, and a Texas resident for at least five years immediately preceding the election. The same qualifications pertain to the lieutenant governor. The constitution also mandates that the governor "shall be installed on the first Tuesday after the organization of the Legislature, or as soon thereafter as practicable."[9] Greg Abbott was sworn in as governor on Tuesday, January 20, 2015. The Texas Legislature is constitutionally responsible for settling any election disputes pertaining to a gubernatorial election.

Compensation

The 1876 constitution stipulated the governor's salary and any raise required a constitutional amendment with the approval of the voters. A 1954 constitutional amendment gave the Legislature the power to determine the governor's annual pay.[10] The Texas governor's salary is $150,000, which is above the average salary ($131,115) for all governors.[11] The lieutenant governor, on the other hand, is paid a salary of a legislator, which is $7,200 a year, plus per diem. The per diem is used to offset the costs of lodging and meals. However, when the governor leaves the state, the lieutenant governor receives a monetary supplement for acting as governor in the governor's absence.

The governor is not the state's top paid chief executive. Chancellors and presidents of some of the state's institutions of higher education (for example, the University of Texas, the University of North Texas, Texas A & M, Texas Tech University, and Stephen F. Austin State University), make well over $200,000 a year. However, the governor receives numerous fringe benefits. He or she is provided an official mansion (in Austin, the state capital) and some other **perks** of the job, including a travel and operating budget, a car, the use of state-owned aircraft, personal security furnished by the Texas Department of Public Safety, and offices and professional staff, such as an executive assistant.

Roles of the Governor

The Texas governor wears different hats and plays various roles. Constitutional rights, statutory authority, informal powers, and symbolic actions provide these roles. The official roles include chief

---

6. Texas Secretary of State at http://elections.sos.state.tx.us/elchist.exe, accessed June, 20, 2012.

7. Texas Secretary of State at http://elections.sos.state.tx.us/elchist.exe, accessed December 16, 2014.

8. See Texas Constitution Article 1, Section 4.

9. Crain and Perkins, *Introduction to Texas Politics*.

10. Ken Collier, Steven Galatas, and Julie Harrelson-Stephens. *Lone Star Politics: Tradition and Transformation in Texas*. (Washington, D.C.: CQ Press, 2012), 109.

11. TheTexasTribune, http://www.texastribune.org/directory/rick-perry, accessed June 14, 2010.

executive, chief legislator, commander in chief, chief of state, and chief intergovernmental diplomat. Some of the informal and symbolic roles include chief of the party and leader of the people.

Informal Characteristics

Since Texas's independence in 1836 all governors have been Caucasian. There have only been two female governors, Miriam Ferguson (1925–1927 and 1933–1935) and Ann Richards (1991–1995). Typically, they are white, Anglo-Saxon protestant (WASP), middle-aged males who assume the office of the governor. This profile is not unusual for a state as conservative as Texas. Most of the time a candidate for governor is a millionaire capable of financing his or her own campaign (or one that has access to vast campaign finance resources). In addition, the average age of governors at the time of their inauguration is 50.03 years old.[12] It is very unlikely that the social status attributes will change when Texas looks to selecting governors.

Formal Powers

As chief executive officer (CEO) of the state of Texas, the governor is allowed to appoint a staff of around 250 employees. These employees are typically loyal to the governor and their appointments are based on patronage. Patronage is where an individual who supported a candidate for public position or is loyal to the candidate is rewarded with a public job offer and appointment. Patronage is also known as the spoils system. They perform a variety of duties and responsibilities including promotion of the governor's legislative agenda, scheduling the governor's commitments, providing the communications of the governor's office, press releases, working on the governor's appointments, and attempting to influence the policy process. Under Governor Abbott there are twenty-one offices that perform these duties and responsibilities (see Table 2.2).

TABLE 2.2 Offices of the Governor	
Appointments Office	Internal Audit
Budget and Policy	Office of Compliance and Monitoring
Commission for Women	Office of the First Lady
Committee on People with Disabilities	Press Office
Constituent Communication	Scheduling and Advance
Criminal Justice Division	Texas Film Commission
Economic Development and Tourism	Texas Military Preparedness Commission
Financial Services	Texas Music Office
General Counsel	Texas Office of State–Federal Relations
Homeland Security Grants Division	Texas Workforce Investment Council
Human Resources	

There are about 350 boards, commissions, and councils in the state of Texas to which the governor makes appointments. Some of them may be familiar like the Stephen F. Austin State University

12. http://texaspolitics.laits.utexas.edu/html/exec/governors/index.html, accessed November 22, 2005.

(SFASU) Board of Regents, the Texas Alcoholic Beverage Commission (TABC), the Texas Parks and Wildlife Commission (TPWC), and the Texas Commission on Environmental Quality (TCEQ). The governor makes over 3,000 appointments to these boards and commissions during a four-year term. People often seek appointment on these boards and the governor and her or his staff solicit nominations. The governor's staff works to ensure the "availability, competence, political acceptability, and support by key interest groups."[13] It is strongly believed and documented[14] that campaign contributions by prospective appointees enhances their chances of serving on a board or commission. Since these positions are coveted, the ability to make appointments to these boards and commissions make the governor politically strong.

Several limitations make the governor constitutionally weak. Appointments require at least a two-thirds vote by the Texas Senate for approval. This requirement protects the minority, as only eleven senators could block an appointment. The governor's staff is aware of the informal **senatorial courtesy** requirement. Prior to the appointment, it is important and almost mandatory for the governor and his staff to gain support of the senator from the home district of a potential appointee. For example, if the potential appointee to a board or commission were from the 3rd Senatorial District here in East Texas, he/she would need the support of current senator Robert Nichols as a senatorial courtesy.

With **six-year overlapping terms,** it often takes governors more than two years in office to get a majority of their appointments on a board or commission.[15] The majority of openings on boards, commissions, and councils occur in January, February, and March of odd-numbered years. For example, Rick Perry, after his first five years in office, appointed all the members to the SFASU Board of Regents with three appointments made in 2001, 2003, and 2005. (Three of the nine regents' terms expire in odd-numbered years.) Governor Abbott appointed three members to the SFASU Board of Regents in 2015 and will appoint three members in 2017 to serve along with three members appointed by Governor Perry. Governor Abbott will make the majority of the appointments until 2017. The governor also appoints a student regent for SFASU. If a vacancy occurs on a board or commission, the governor can fill it regardless of the expiration date. These six-year overlapping terms make the governor constitutionally weak.

If an appointment to a board, commission, or council does not meet the expectations of the governor the appointment can be removed from the position with a two-thirds vote in the Texas Senate. This constitutional limitation weakens the appointment powers of the governor. It would be difficult for a governor to get the senatorial votes that have the willingness to remove an appointment.

In addition, boards and commissions with enormous policy impact are elected, making the governor constitutionally weak. For example, the members of the State Board of Education and the Texas Railroad Commission are elected. The State Board of Education nominates a person to the governor to be the Commissioner of Education. The Texas Railroad Commission regulates the oil and natural gas industry (see the next chapter, The Texas Bureaucracy).

The Texas governor lacks budgetary powers that governors of other states possess. This makes the Texas governor constitutionally weak. In Texas, **the Legislative Budget Board**, which includes the lieutenant governor and the Speaker of the House, has more influence over the budget than the governor. This lack of constitutional authority, combined with the requirement to submit a biennial budget, may have led Governor Perry to introduce a zero-base budget in January of 2003. Perry's

---

13. Thomas R. Dye with Tucker Gibson, Jr. and Clay Robison, *Politics in America Texas Edition, 5th ed.* (Upper Saddle River, NJ, 2005), 807.

14. Gary M. Halter. "Government and Politics of Texas: A Comparative View". In *The American Democracy; Texas, 7th ed.* by Thomas E. Patterson. (Boston: McGraw Hill, 2005), 165.

15. Ibid., 165.

TABLE 2.3	Line-Item Veto Power of the Governor	
Year	**Budget (millions)***	**Line-Item Amount**
2016–17	$209,400	$295 million
2014–15	$200,421	Not Available
2012–13	$190,755	$0**
2010–11	$187,517	$386 million
2008–09	$172,131	$647 million
2006–07	$142,745	$1.7 billion
2004-05	$126,634	$81 million
2002–03	$115,916	$556 million

*Legislative Budget Board, Fiscal Size-up 2014–15 Biennium, http://www.lbb.state.tx.us/Documents/Publications/Fiscal_SizeUp/Fiscal_SizeUp.pdf p.41, accessed December 17, 2015.
** The Governor's Veto Proclamation for the 2012–13 General Appropriations Bill did not have any fiscal impact because the only items vetoed were for contingency appropriations for bills that <u>did not pass</u>. E-mail communication with Legislative Budget Board, June 22, 2012.

budget was for $0.00 because he believed that all state spending should be reexamined. However, the governor does have **line-item veto** power over legislative appropriations (see Table 3.3). Line-item veto power allows the governor to delete specific spending items while leaving the vast majority of an appropriations bill untouched. In June of 2015, Governor Abbott line-item vetoed an appropriation of $500,000 for 2016 and $500,000 for 2017 for the Waters of East Texas (WET) Center to be located at Stephen F. Austin State University. Governor Abbott noted that "If the WET Center is a priority, the University may use its appropriation for institutional enhancement, leverage public-private partnerships, or allocate other resources for this purpose."[16] The line-item veto power makes the Texas governor politically strong.

Legislative Powers

The governor can also propose bills to the Texas Legislature. In 1997, Governor Bush proposed a bill called "Cutting Texas Taxes." This bill did not pass largely because the cutting of property taxes, supported by landowners and landlords, was to be replaced with an increase in the state sales tax from 6.25 to 6.75 percent. The majority of Texans are opposed to tax increases, even if they are designed to offset a tax decrease. The biggest legislative power of the governor is that she or he can **sign bills into law**. During the 84th session (2015) of the Texas Legislature, Governor Abbott signed over 1,200 bills into law (see Table 2.4). Most of these signings are done without a lot of fanfare; yet, they impact the lives of Texans. The bills signed by Governor Abbott included the state budget, early education initiatives, an open carry bill for concealed handgun license holders, campus carry by concealed handgun license holders with the caveat that lets college presidents designate "gun-free zones," and a bill prohibiting cities (like Denton) from banning hydraulic fracturing.

The governor's legislative powers also include **veto power,** which is one of the most influential legislative tools to encourage the Texas Legislature to pass favorable bills. The governor can veto a bill passed by the Legislature. During the 77th session of the Texas Legislature, Governor Perry vetoed a record number eighty-two bills (see Table 2.4). With the large volume of bills signed, those

---

16. Proclamation by the Governor of the State of Texas, June 20, 2015.

TABLE 2.4 The Governor's Imprint on Legislation		
Year	**Bills Signed**	**Bills Vetoed**
2015	1,204	42
2013	1,573	26
2011	1,458	24
2009	1,414	36
2007	1,651	54
2005	1,555	19
2003	1,583	48
2001	1,809	82

vetoed often receive scant attention from the media and the public. Governor Abbott vetoed HB 1363 as he believed it would not have been in the best interest of the offender or the people of Texas. HB 1363 would have changed the criminal offenses for a person receiving a fee for prostitution and a person paying a fee for prostitution. First convictions for either offense would have remained a class B misdemeanor (up to 180 days in jail and/or a maximum fine of $2,000). Without the governor's veto, second and third convictions would have been class B misdemeanors instead of class A misdemeanors (up to one year in jail and/or a maximum fine of $4,000). Fourth, fifth, and sixth offenses would have been class A misdemeanors instead of state jail felonies (up to two years in jail and/or a maximum fine of $10,000) as under current law. The Texas Legislature, which may be controlled by the governor's party, will not find it politically expedient or practical to attempt to override the governor's vote with a two-thirds majority in the House and Senate of the Texas Legislature.

Governors often give messages that have an impact on legislation. When a governor first takes office he/she delivers an **inaugural address** to citizens, interest groups, and legislators. This address typically occurs when the new governor has great popular support since winning the statewide election the previous year.

The governor also delivers a **State of the State Message**. This message coincides with the beginning of a session of the Texas Legislature in odd-numbered years. The governor can use this message to direct the legislative agenda.

In the 2013 State of the State speech to members of the Texas Legislature, Governor Perry discussed job growth and business creation, other states imitating Texas (e.g., Louisiana attempting to eliminate the state income tax), financial issues keeping Texas a low-tax state, directives (e.g., use of the Rainy Day Fund) for infrastructure (water and transportation) needs, continued education improvements, and the role of state agencies like TxDOT (Texas Department of Transportation), DPS (Department of Public Safety), and TEA (Texas Education Agency). Governor Perry ended the address stating: "Thank you, God bless you and, through you, may He continue to bless the Great State of Texas."[17]

In the 2015 State of the State speech to members of the Texas Legislature, Governor Abbott noted that Texas leads the nation in economic growth because of its greatest natural resource—the people of Texas—who've built a strong and diversified economy. Governor Abbott discussed five emergencies: early education, higher education research initiatives, transportation funding, border security funding, and ethics reforms. In addition, Governor Abbott called for the reduction of the business

---

17. Texas Governor Rick Perry's 2013 State of the State Speech in Governing: The States and Localities, http://www.governing.com/news/state/texas-perry-2013-speech.html, accessed July 27, 2013.

franchise tax and property tax reduction as part of his effort to constrain the size of government. He also advocated expanding liberty in Texas by stating he would sign an open carry of handguns law.[18]

The governor can call **special sessions** of the Texas Legislature. This power makes the governor politically strong in the legislative process but can also become a liability. The governor sets the agenda for these sessions, which last thirty days. In 2003, Governor Perry called four special sessions after the 78th regular session of the Texas Legislature to resolve the redistricting issue for the US House of Representatives seats. Governor Perry called two special sessions in 2005 after the 79th regular session of the Texas Legislature failed to resolve the school finance dilemma. Since the school finance system was not reformed during these sessions and was found unconstitutional by the Texas Supreme Court, Governor Perry called a third special session in 2006. Governor Perry called a special session after the 81st (2009) regular session to continue state agencies subject to sunset review (see next chapter), the issuance of general obligation bonds by the Texas Transportation Commission, and to extend the date when the Texas Department of Transportation's authority to enter comprehensive development agreements expire.[19]

After the 82nd regular session of the Texas Legislature in 2011, Governor Perry called a special session to approve the budget and contain health care costs. After the special session started, he added a ban on "sanctuary cities" and a ban on "intrusive" airport security screenings to the agenda—both measures failed to gain legislative approval. The budget was approved and signed by Governor Perry.

After the 83rd regular session of the Texas Legislature in 2013, Governor Perry called the first special session to adopt interim redistricting plans ordered by a federal court, which was approved and signed by the governor. Three other issues—abortion restrictions, juvenile justice, and transportation funding—that were on the agenda for the first session did not gain approval of the legislature, so Governor Perry called a second special session. The abortion restrictions bill was approved and signed by Governor Perry and the juvenile justice bill was approved during the second special session. Governor Perry had to call a third special session to receive approval of the transportation funding bill.

Typically, legislators dislike being called into a special session during the summer months after a regular session or in even-numbered years. The power to call a special session makes the governor politically strong. The threat to call a special session may force the legislature to work on the governor's priorities during the regular session. When the governor must continually call special sessions and issues are not resolved they can become a liability for the governor as his or her leadership can be questioned and approval ratings might decline.

Judicial

Although most judges in Texas are elected, the governor is in a unique position to make **judicial appointments** when a vacancy occurs through death or resignation of a state judge, or when a new court is established. The majority of these appointments are to state district courts. These courts have criminal and civil jurisdictions. On the criminal side they hear cases that involve felonies and on the civil side they can hear cases that involve millions of dollars in alleged damages. Judges appointed by the governor become incumbents and typically win the next election. About 50 percent of the Texas judges and justices first serve as gubernatorial appointments to fill vacancies. This judicial power makes the governor politically strong.

18. Texas Governor Greg Abbott's 2015 State of the State Speech, http://gov.texas.gov/news/speech/20659, accessed July 10, 2015.
19. Office of the Governor, Rick Perry, http://governor.state.tx.us/news/proclamation/12758/ accessed, June 12, 2010.

The Board of Pardons and Paroles can release felons early without the governor's consent. The 1876 constitution originally granted the governor the power of pardon; however, in 1936 when the Fergusons (Governors Miriam and James, 1915–1917) were accused of being influenced financially for pardons a constitutional amendment created the Board of Pardons and Paroles. This amendment weakened the power of governors.[20] The governor has political influence over this board by making appointments to this seven-member board. Without the approval of the board, the governor can grant a thirty-day stay in the execution of a convicted capital murderer. "The governor, on recommendation of the board, can grant a full pardon to a criminal, a conditional pardon, or the commutation of a death sentence to life imprisonment."[21]

Conclusions

Over the past decade, the visibility of the Texas Governor has increased. When George W. Bush decided to run for President of the United States, political scientists often joked, "Why does he want to take a political step down?" The joke suggested that the Governor of Texas is the top executive position in the nation; in reality this is not true. Governor Perry had a failed attempt to become president. The governor plays many roles and has executive, legislative, and judicial powers. The various roles and informal and symbolic powers make the Texas Governor politically strong; however, the powers provided to other members of the plural executive, the Texas Legislature, and various boards, commissions, and councils, make the governor constitutionally weak. We predict that Governor Abbott will be politically strong and constitutionally weak.

Key Terms

Plural Executive
Off-Years
Four-Year Term
Perks
Senatorial Courtesy
Six-Year Overlapping Terms
Legislative Budget Board
Line-Item Veto
Sign Bills into Law
Veto Power
Inaugural Address
State of the State Message
Special Sessions
Judicial Appointments

---

20. Collier, Galatas, and Harrelson-Stephens, 104.

21. Thomas R. Dye with Tucker Gibson, Jr. and Clay Robison, *Politics in America Texas Edition*, 5th ed. 2005. (Upper Saddle River, NJ), 808.

Exercise 2.1 ■ Multiple Choice

1. Texas governors are considered weak:
   a. in terms of constitutional powers.
   b. because they must frequently visit medical doctors for health reasons.
   c. in terms of political powers.
   d. because the Texas Legislature is more powerful.

2. Candidates for Texas governor:
   a. have a lieutenant governor as a running mate.
   b. are elected in "off-years" when the country is not electing the US president.
   c. are not allowed to run a political party ticket.
   d. must be of Protestant religion and believe in the Supreme Being.

3. In order to be elected governor, one must be a US citizen and _____ years of age.
   a. 21
   b. 25
   c. 30
   d. 35

4. The governor of Texas has a:
   a. two-year term, with no limit on terms.
   b. two-year term, with a four-term limit.
   c. four-year term, with no limit on terms.
   d. four-year term, limited to two terms in lifetime.

5. The pay of the Texas governor is the highest among all state employees.
   a. True
   b. False

6. The _____ is next in line of succession behind the governor.
   a. speaker of the Texas House of Representatives
   b. attorney general
   c. lieutenant governor
   d. comptroller

7. If a state district judge would resign, the immediate vacancy would be filled by an appointment from the:
   a. Texas Supreme Court
   b. Texas governor
   c. Texas attorney general
   d. the people after a special election
   e. the State Bar Association

8. The governor of Texas appoints the secretary of state.
   a. True
   b. False

9. The governor's appointment power is considered constitutionally weak because:
   a. they cannot appoint their own staffs.
   b. appointments require a two-thirds vote of the Texas Senate for approval.
   c. it takes a constitutional amendment to remove a board, commission, or council member.
   d. very few Texans seek to become members of boards, commissions, and councils.
   e. There are only seventy-five boards, commissions, and councils in Texas.

10. The legislative powers of the governor include:
    a. the power to set the agenda for a regular legislative session.
    b. appointing the lieutenant governor.
    c. the power to set the agenda for a special legislative session.
    d. invoking senatorial courtesy which forces quick legislative action on executive orders in the Texas Senate.
    e. appointing the Speaker of the House.

Exercise 2.2   ■   Analytical Essay

Log on to the Office of the Governor website (http://www.governor.state.tx.us/). Write an essay where you explain the governor's position on a policy issue. What political challenges does the governor confront? Do you agree or disagree with the governor's position?

Exercise 2.3　■　Research Exercise

Log on to the Organizations Section of the Office of the Governor website (http://www.governor.state.tx.us/organization). Select one of the twenty-one offices. Write a short essay explaining why you think this organization is important to the State of Texas.

CHAPTER 3

The Texas Bureaucracy

Dr. Richard J. Herzog

The Texas Bureaucracy has a great impact on the lives of Texans. A **bureaucracy** is a way to organize people to perform work. Many discussions of the "ideal-type" bureaucracy are accredited to Max Weber (1862–1920), a German sociologist and political economist. The **characteristics of the bureaucracy** include a hierarchical authority structure, a chain of command/approval, task specialization and the division of labor, merit systems, formalized rules, neutral decision-making, and the absence of politics. The Texas Bureaucracy employed an average of 310,959.1 full-time equivalent (FTE) employees in state agencies and higher education institutions in fiscal year 2014[1] and has several characteristics of a bureaucracy.

Most state agencies discussed in this chapter have organization charts which detail the divisions, programs, and personnel (i.e., the hierarchical authority structure). Chain of command goes from the top of an organization to the bottom. For example, to implement a hurricane evacuation plan, the commands would flow top-down. Conversely, prior to a new initiative taking place, like a new undergraduate program, approval would have to be given by an academic department, at the bottom, all the way to the Texas Higher Education Coordinating Board at the top.

The mission of each agency will suggest the type of task specialization and the division of labor within the organization. Within each agency, employees with expertise (e.g., engineering, teaching, systems analyzing) are called to conduct operations.

Texas Bureaucracy does not have a centralized personnel system; however, many agencies hire, promote, and retain employees based on merit. Merit is based on qualifications and performance.

Each agency discussed below will have several formalized rules. These rules may include determining which purchased items are assessed sales tax. For example, fast-food is assessed a sales tax and newspapers are not assessed a sales tax.

---

1. State Auditor's Office, *A Summary Report on Full-time Equivalent State Employees for Fiscal Year 2014* Report Number 15-705. February, 2015. Note the fiscal year in Texas is from September 1 to August 31.

When a state employee utilizes neutral decision-making, actions are undertaken without racial, gender, ethnic, or religious bias or preference. For example, a Department of Public Safety officer would issue a speeding ticket to anyone exceeding 90 mph (miles per hour), regardless of their personal characteristics.

By design, Texas Bureaucracy fails the ideal bureaucracy criterion of the absence of politics. Since the heads of many agencies are elected, appointed by the governor, or selected by boards and commissions appointed by the governor, this guarantees that "who you know" is often more important than "what you know."

The Constitution of 1876

Article IV covers the Executive Department in Texas and identifies the top seven executive branch officials. It states, "The executive department of the State shall consist of a governor, who shall be the chief executive officer of the State, a lieutenant-governor, secretary of state, comptroller of public accounts, treasurer, commissioner of the general land office and attorney general." This chapter will not discuss the governor (see previous chapter, "The Texas Governor: Politically Strong, Constitutionally Weak") or the lieutenant governor (see Chapter 1, "The Texas Legislature"). This chapter discusses the attorney general, comptroller, secretary of state, commissioner of the general land office, in addition to the commissioner of agriculture. These offices are collectively referred to as the **plural executive**. This chapter also discusses the Texas Council on Environmental Quality, the Texas Department of Parks and Wildlife, the State Board of Education, the Texas Education Agency, the Railroad Commission of Texas, and the Sunset Advisory Commission. The conclusions end the chapter.

Personnel and Budgets

Table 3.1 list the agencies discussed in this chapter with the number of full-time equivalent (FTE) employees and expenditures. One decimal place is used by the State Auditor to accurately count the number of full-time employees. The number of employees is average for fiscal year 2015 that ended on August 31, 2015. The Fiscal Year 2016 expenditure information presented in Table 3.1 will be close to the Fiscal Year 2017 expenditures that started on September 1, 2016.

TABLE 3.1 Number of Employees and Expenditure		
Agency	**Fiscal Year 2015 Employees**	**Fiscal Year 2016 Expenditures**
Office of the Attorney General	4,092.10	$911,849,389.44
Texas Comptroller of Public Accounts	2,771.50	$333,081,855.95
Secretary of State	194.80	$38,969,888.28
Texas Department of Agriculture	615.30	$634,797,891.77
General Land Office	621.10	$2,881,042,282.60
Commission on Environmental Quality	2,689.20	$477,623,219.52
Department of Parks and Wildlife	2,984	$377,499,504.46
Texas Education Agency	832.40	$28,334,427,950.26
Railroad Commission of Texas	764.40	$83,649,786.71
Sunset Advisory Commission	27	$2,999,556.72
Source: State Auditor and State Comptroller		

The Office of the Attorney General

The Texas Attorney General is selected in a statewide election every four years (2018, 2022, and 2026). The attorney general represents the State of Texas on civil matters, provides consumer protection, heads child support enforcement, and provides legal opinions to state and local officials.

In the mid-1990s, Texas Attorney General Dan Morales sued the tobacco companies for not telling the truth about the manipulation of nicotine amounts and addictions, and for reimbursement of Medicaid expenses paid by the State of Texas for smoking-related illnesses.[2] The settlement with the tobacco companies was for $15.3 billion to be paid to the state over twenty-five years. Attorney General Morales noted, ``Our lawsuit asserts that the history of this industry has been rooted in a concerted, decades-long conspiracy to conceal the truth about tobacco.''[3]

The Office of the Attorney General provides consumer protection by filing lawsuits against businesses that violate state law. These violations are brought to the attention of the Office of the Attorney General when consumers file complaints. Consumer protection laws cover car repairs, credit cards, prescription drugs, and tenant rights.[4]

The Child Support Division (CSD) provides services to parents free of charge as stipulated by federal law. The US Government and the State of Texas provide funding for these services. The CSD locates parents, establishes paternity, and enforces child support orders on a case-by-case basis. In fiscal year 2014, the Child Support Division had 1,462,517 open cases.[5] A case could have multiple children associated with it. About 80 percent of parents pay child support toward their court ordered obligations, but they may not pay the entire amount owed. The balance owed is called the arrears. In state fiscal year 2015, the CSD collected and distributed over $3.8 billion in child support payments.[6] The amount arrears, the amount owed to a custodial parent or the government, is estimated to be over $9 billion in Texas and over $106 billion nationwide.

In addition, the Office of the Attorney General provides legal opinions to state and local government officials. For example, the Office of the Attorney General is requested by the State Legislature to rule on bills that would allow casino gambling in the state. The attorney general's opinions are that it will take a **constitutional amendment** to allow casino gambling in Texas. To amend the Texas Constitution, it would take a two-thirds vote of the members of the House of Representatives and Senate to get the amendment on a November ballot that must be approved by a majority of the voters.

Texas Comptroller of Public Accounts

The Texas Comptroller of Public Accounts (known as the comptroller) is chosen in a statewide election every four years (2018, 2022, and 2026). The comptroller is the chief tax collector for the State of Texas. The office "serves the state by collecting more than 50 separate taxes, fees and assessments, including local sales taxes collected on behalf of more than 1,400 cities, counties and other local governments around the state"[7] (see Table 3.2). Most of these taxes, fees, and assessments affect your lives by collecting your money and then provides state goods and services. In addition,

---

2. Other states also filed lawsuits. See *The Washington Post,* May 1, 1996.
3. *The Wisconsin State Journal* (Madison, WI), January 17, 1998.
4. Attorney General of Texas, https://www.texasattorneygeneral.gov/cpd/consumer-protection.
5. U.S. Department of Health and Human Services, Office of Child Support Enforcement, http://www.acf.hhs.gov/programs/css/resource/status-of-automated-child-support-systems, accessed July 18, 2015.
6. U.S. Department of Health and Human Services, Office of Child Support Enforcement, Preliminary Report FY 2015, http://www.acf.hhs.gov/css/resource/fy-2015-preliminary-report, accessed November 1, 2016.
7. Texas Comptroller of Public Accounts, http://comptroller.texas.gov/taxes/.

TABLE 3.2 Selected State of Texas Taxes and Rates	
Tax	**Rate**
Cigarette	$1.41 per 20-pack
Fireworks	2 percent in addition to sales tax
Gasoline	$.20 per gallon
Hotel Occupancy	6 percent to the cost of the room
Mixed Beverage	6.7 percent of gross receipts in addition to sales tax
Sales	6.25 percent
Note: Local options can bring the total sales tax to 8.25 percent	

the comptroller administers the deposits of state monies, pays the expenses of the state, makes revenue forecasts, and certifies revenue for the biennial state budget.

The comptroller makes deposits of state money into interest bearing accounts as the state will have more money than is required to pay expenses. With modern financial administration, most state agencies are able to pay their own expenses, but the ultimate authority is with the state comptroller. The comptroller provides a **biennial revenue estimate** to the Texas Legislature before the legislative sessions. This estimate requires complex revenue forecasting. After the budget is approved by the Texas Legislature, the comptroller must certify that the revenue will be available. This is required as Texas follows the principle of **pay-as-you-go**. Pay-as-you-go means that the state has a balanced budget where revenues match expenditures.

Secretary of State

The Texas Secretary of State is appointed by the governor, confirmed by a two-thirds vote in the Senate, and "serves at the pleasure of the Governor."[8] The secretary of state enforces election laws, tabulates election returns, and attempts to increase voter participation. This position has been an important liaison with the affairs between Texas and Mexico.

The secretary of state must enforce numerous election laws. The laws govern various officials in the election process including county chairs of political parties, county clerks, tax assessor-collectors/voter registrars, elections administrators, city secretaries/clerks, and procedures specific to school districts and various other political subdivisions (e.g., cities and hospital districts). Additional laws detail the placing of the candidates on the ballot, training for poll workers, procedures for recounts, and early voting requirements.

After an election, the results are submitted to the Office of the Secretary of State and certified. Election results are posted on the agency's web page to provide **transparency,** which allows the public to view the results of governance. After 2012, it was clear that Texas was a "red" or Republican Party state as Mitt Romney and Paul Ryan gained 57.16 percent of the vote (4,569,843), and President Barack Obama and Vice President Joe Biden received 41.38 percent of the vote (3,308,124).

To increase voter participation, the secretary of state promotes Project V.O.T.E. (Voters of Tomorrow through Education). This project is designed for grades K through 12 to educate students about voting so they will become voters in the future.

---

8. Texas Secretary of State, http://www.sos.state.tx.us/about/index.shtml, accessed July 18, 2015.

As the governor's liaison for the Texas Border and Mexican Affairs, the secretary of state has key responsibilities:

- Accompanying the governor when meeting with Mexican officials
- Monitoring and advising the governor's office and other agencies on issues affecting Texas–Mexico relations
- Working with Mexican federal, state, and local officials on issues affecting Texas, Mexico, and the border region
- Representing the governor at international meetings and in planning the Border Governors Conference
- Monitoring state and federal legislation on border issues[9]

Commissioner of Agriculture

The Commissioner of Agriculture is selected in a statewide election every four years (2018, 2022, and 2026). The Texas Department of Agriculture enforces the Texas Administrative Code, which details a variety of rules and regulations covering fuel quality, pesticides, egg laws, and handling perishable commodities. The Department of Agriculture certifies the accuracy of pumps and scales. Therefore, when you purchase five gallons of gas or three pounds of bananas, you have a reasonable assurance that the pumps and scales are accurate, if they have been certified.

The Texas Department of Agriculture follows the slogan GO TEXAN to promote the products, culture, and communities that call Texas home.[10] The GO TEXAN programs include products, communities, restaurants, and special programs. By searching the GO TEXAN products web page, domestic and international sales of beef, candy, shrimp, and wine are promoted, making it easy for wholesale purchasers to locate products. The Certified Retirement Program was established to retain and recruit retirees to Texas. Nacogdoches County was one of the first Certified Retirement Communities in the state. To become a Certified Retirement Community officials of the city or county have to submit an application that details the desirability of their community to retirees.[11] "The GO TEXAN stamp of approval ensures each certified community has demonstrated through its application that it can meet the living, employment/volunteer, health, entertainment, education and safety needs of its citizens and visitors all the things that make Texas a great place to retire." The GO TEXAN Restaurant Program is new and supports "chefs and owners committed to serving locally produced items—from shrimp to wine to seasonal vegetables."[12] Special programs under the GO TEXAN slogan include the State Fair, Wildlife Initiatives, Pick Texas, Square Meals, International Marketing, Texas Department of Agriculture Market Reports, and the Texas Agricultural Statistical Services. Overall, the Texas Department of Agriculture helps to promote and ensure the quality of Texas' products, restaurants, and communities.

Land Commissioner

The Land Commissioner is chosen in a statewide election every four years (2018, 2022, and 2026). The Land Commissioner manages over thirteen million acres of revenue generating state land.

9. Texas Secretary of State, http://sos.state.tx.us/border/index.shtml, accessed July 18, 2015.

10. Texas Department of Agriculture, http://www.gotexan.org/, accessed July 18, 2015.

11. Texas Department of Agriculture, http://www.retireintexas.org/Home/CertifiedRetirementCommunities.aspx, accessed June 25, 2012

12. Texas Department of Agriculture, http://www.gotexanrestaurantroundup.com/Home.aspx, accessed June 25, 2012

Revenue is collected by awarding leases and mineral rights. State land is located throughout the state including East Texas and coastal areas where state land extends 10.3 miles from the shoreline.[13] "The General Land Office leases state land for a variety of purposes, including oil and gas production, commercial development, and sustainable energy development. Many of the state land leases benefit the Permanent School Fund, an endowment fund for public school education in Texas."[14] Various programs like Adopt-A-Beach, the Coastal Erosion Planning and Response Act, Texas Farm & Ranch Lands, and Oil Spill Prevention & Response work to protect our natural resources. In addition, the Texas General Land Office seeks to provide renewable energy leadership. Renewable energy sources include "wind, water (hydro), wave power, biomass, geothermal, and solar."[15] "In 2006, Texas surpassed California to become the No. 1 producer of wind energy in the United States. Currently, Texas leads the nation in installed wind capacity, at 8,361 MW [megawatts], or enough electricity to power approximately 2,500,000 homes."[16]

Other Selected Agencies

Texas Council on Environmental Quality

The Texas Council on Environmental Quality (TCEQ) has three commissioners who are appointed by the governor. The mission of the council is "to protect our state's human and natural resources consistent with sustainable economic development. Our goal is clean air, clean water, and the safe management of waste."[17] State attempts to have sustainable economic development and clean air, clean water, and the safe management of waste are often delicate balancing acts.

Texas Department of Parks and Wildlife

A nine-member commission heads the Texas Parks and Wildlife Department (TPWD). The governor appoints each commissioner. The TPWD's mission is to manage and conserve the natural and cultural resources of Texas and to provide hunting, fishing, and outdoor recreation opportunities for the use and enjoyment of present and future generations.[18] On the parks' side of the department, the TPWD maintains and promotes the use of state parks, historic sites, state natural areas, wildlife management areas, and visitors' centers. The wildlife side of the department includes managing fishing and hunting regulations and opportunities. The TPWD governs fishing license requirements, monitors aquatic species, and provides a variety of programs, in addition to fisheries management. The TPWD regulates boat registration and titling requirements, provides boater education, and tries to make the boating public aware of the laws. The TPWD oversees the hunting license requirements, the seasons and bag limits for various animals, hunter education, and the management of wildlife areas. The TPWD also addresses a host of additional land and water issues.

13. Texas General Land Office, http://www.glo.texas.gov/glo_news/agency-facts/glo-fact-sheet.html, accessed July 18, 2015

14. Ibid.

15. Texas General Land Office, http://www.glo.state.tx.us/energy/sustain/, accessed June 4, 2010.

16. Ibid.

17. Texas Commission on Environmental Quality, http://www.tceq.texas.gov/about, accessed July 18, 2015.

18. Texas Parks and Wildlife Department, http://www.tpwd.state.tx.us/business/about/mission, accessed July 18, 2105.

State Board of Education and the Texas Education Agency

The State Board of Education has fifteen elected members from different regions of the state and one member is appointed chair by the governor. The State Board of Education oversees, monitors, and guides the Texas Education Agency (TEA). The mission of the agency "is to provide leadership, guidance and resources to help schools meet the educational needs of all students."[19] The governor appoints the Commissioner of Education. Under the leadership of the Commissioner, the TEA:

- manages the textbook adoption process;
- oversees development of the statewide curriculum;
- administers the statewide assessment program;
- administers a data collection system on public school students, staff, and finances;
- rates school districts under the statewide accountability system;
- operates research and information programs;
- monitors for compliance with federal guidelines; and
- serves as a fiscal agent for the distribution of state and federal funds.[20]

Railroad Commission of Texas

The Railroad Commission of Texas (RRC) has three elected commissioners. The title of the Railroad Commission of Texas has been a misnomer or a name falsely applied. The RRC has "primary regulatory jurisdiction over the oil and natural gas industry, pipeline transporters, natural gas and hazardous liquid pipeline industry, natural gas utilities, the LP-gas industry, and coal and uranium surface mining operations. It is also responsible for research and education to promote the use of LP-gas [liquid petroleum gas, a.k.a. propane] as an alternative fuel in Texas."[21] LP stands for liquefied petroleum or propane. Since 2005, the safety oversight of the railroad industry is with the Texas Department of Transportation and the RCC does not have regulatory authority.

Sunset Advisory Commission

In 1977, the Texas Legislature created the Sunset Advisory Commission with twelve legislative members to identify and eliminate waste, duplication, and inefficiency in more than 130 Texas state agencies.[22] Universities and courts are not subject to **sunset review.**

The basic question the Sunset Advisory Commission asks is, "Does the agency or program need to exist?"

> [1st] Sunset staff performs extensive research and analysis to evaluate the need for, performance of, and improvements to the agency under review. [2nd] The Sunset Advisory Commission conducts a public hearing to take testimony on the staff report and the agency overall. Later the Commission meets again to vote on which changes to recommend to the full Legislature. [3rd] The full Legislature considers Sunset recommendations and makes final determinations.[23]

---

19. Texas Education Agency, http://www.tea.state.tx.us/index4.aspx?id=3793, accessed June 25, 2012.
20. Ibid.
21. Railroad Commission of Texas, http://www.rrc.state.tx.us/about/faqs/rrcjurisdictions.php, accessed June 25, 2012.
22. Texas Sunset Advisory Commission, http://www.sunset.texas.gov/about-us, accessed July 18, 2015.
23. Texas Sunset Advisory Commission, https://www.sunset.texas.gov/how-sunset-works, accessed July 20, 2015.

TABLE 3.3 Scheduled Agency Reviews 2016–2017 Cycle*
▪ Bar of Texas, State
▪ Central Colorado River Authority
▪ Chiropractic Examiners, Texas Board of
▪ Counselors, Texas State Board of Examiners of Professionals
▪ Dental Examiners, State Board of
▪ Employees Retirement System of Texas, Board of Trustees of
▪ Law Examiners, Board of
▪ Marriage and Family Therapists, Texas State Board of Examiners of
▪ Medical Board, Texas
▪ Nursing, Texas Board of
▪ Occupational Therapy Examiners, Texas Board of
▪ Optometry Board, Texas
▪ Pal Duro River Authority of Texas
▪ Pharmacy, Texas State Board of
▪ Physical Therapy and Occupational Therapy Examiners, Executive Council of
▪ Physical Therapy Examiners, Texas Board of
▪ Podiatric Medical Examiners, Texas State Board of
▪ Psychologists, Texas State Board of Examiners of
▪ Railroad Commission of Texas
▪ Social Worker Examiners, Texas State Board of
▪ Sulphur River Basin Authority
▪ Transportation, Texas Department of
▪ Upper Colorado River Authority
▪ Veterinary Medical Examiners, State Board of
https://www.sunset.texas.gov/reviews-and-reports accessed, November 2, 2016.

If the legislature does not vote to continue the agency or program, the "sun will set" and the agency and program will begin a year of termination operations. During the 2016–2017 cycle, the Sunset Advisory Commission will conduct twenty-four reviews (see Table 3.3). The 84th (2015) Legislature enacted fourteen Sunset bills that "will result in more than $34 million in savings and revenue gains over the next two years by eliminating waste, duplication, and inefficiency in state government."[24] The most significant change abolishes the Department of Assistive and Rehabilitative Services (DARS) in 2016 and the Department of Aging and Disability Services (DADS) in 2017, consolidating their functions into the Health and Human Services Commission (HHSC).[25]

24. Texas Sunset Advisory Commission, *Final Results of Sunset Reviews* 2014–2015, (July 2015), 1.
25. Ibid.

Conclusions

The Texas Bureaucracy with elected heads, boards, and commissions of agencies is often referred to as a plural executive, as no single executive (like the governor in other states) has complete control. In a state as large as Texas, the bureaucracy is vast and must be judged on criteria like transparency, accountability, and a high level of performance that are different from the characteristics of a bureaucracy that introduced the chapter. Transparency is excellent as the research and information for this chapter was obtained on the World Wide Web. The plural executive places Texans in a unique position to hold many public officials accountable at the ballot box. The continued efforts by the secretary of state to increase voter participation are important. In general, it is believed that many state agencies are high performing and others appear to need performance improvement. Attempts to evaluate the performance of state agencies center on the achievement of missions discussed in this chapter.

Key Terms

Bureaucracy
Characteristics of the Bureaucracy
Article IV
Plural Executive
Constitutional Amendment
Biennial Revenue Estimate
Pay-as-you-go
Transparency
Sunset Review

Exercise 3.1　■　Multiple Choice

1. If Texas has an "ideal type" of bureaucracy it would be characterized by:
   a. partisan decision-making.
   b. cross-training.
   c. selection of employees based on merit.
   d. flexible operating procedures.

2. Which agency has the most employees?
   a. Office of the Attorney General
   b. Texas Comptroller of Public Accounts
   c. Texas Department of Parks and Wildlife
   d. Texas Education Agency

3. If Texans have concerns about a consumer protection law they would contact the:
   a. Office of the Attorney General.
   b. Comptroller of Public Accounts.
   c. Governor's Office.
   d. Secretary of State's Office.
   e. Lieutenant Governor's Office.

4. Which rate of taxation for the State of Texas is correct?
   a. The gasoline tax is $.50 per gallon.
   b. The state fireworks tax is 8 percent plus sales tax.
   c. The state hotel occupancy tax is 2 percent.
   d. The mixed drink beverage tax is 6.7 percent of gross receipts plus sales tax.
   e. A regular package of cigarettes is taxed at 20 cents per pack.

5. Efforts to increase voter participation are the responsibility of the:
   a. Office of the Attorney General.
   b. Comptroller of Public Accounts.
   c. Governor's Office.
   d. Secretary of State's Office.
   e. Lieutenant Governor's Office.

6. The GO TEXAN slogan sponsored by the Texas Department of Agriculture is designed to promote:
   a. commercial transportation of fresh fruits and vegetables on state highways.
   b. out-of-state investments by Texas agribusinesses to escape high taxation.
   c. the products, culture, and communities that call Texas home.
   d. the highest standards of beef, eggs, poultry, and seafood, and dairy products in Texas.

7. Which of the following has an elected council, commission, or board?
   a. Texas Council on Environmental Quality
   b. Texas Department of Parks and Wildlife
   c. State Board of Education
   d. Sunset Review Commission

8. Which agency has primary jurisdiction over the oil and natural gas industry?
   a. Texas General Land Office
   b. Texas Council on Environmental Quality
   c. Railroad Commission of Texas
   d. Public Utility Commission of Texas

9. Which commission attempts to eliminate waste, duplication, and inefficiency in Texas government agencies?
   a. Sunset Review Commission
   b. Beat Waste Commission
   c. Performance Review Commission
   d. Beat Bureaucracy Commission

10. The Texas Bureaucracy with elected heads, boards, and commissions of agencies is often referred to as the _____ executive.
   a. fragmented
   b. split
   c. plural
   d. accountable
   e. transparent

Exercise 3.2 ■ Analytical Essay

Log on to one of the agencies discussed in this chapter (see http://www.tsl.state.tx.us/apps/lrs/
agencies/index.html). Discuss three characteristics of the "ideal-type" bureaucracy found in this
agency. Your essay should cover this directive, be well written, provide proper citation if necessary,
and be between 300 and 500 words. Include a word count at the end of your essay.

Exercise 3.3 ■ Research and Evaluation Exercise

Pick a Texas state agency from the Texas State Library and Archives Commission (see http://www.tsl.state.tx.us/apps/lrs/agencies/index.html) and discuss its mission and why you think the sun should or should not set on this agency. Would you like to work for this agency? Your essay should cover this directive, be well written, provide proper citation if necessary, and be between 300 and 500 words.

CHAPTER 4

The Texas Judiciary

Michael Tkacik

Texas has one of the most complex legal systems in the United States. The system is complex even from an attorney's point of view. The judicial system in Texas is decentralized, with multiple courts sometimes having responsibility for the same type of case. Some courts also have both original and appellate jurisdiction. Moreover, most judges in Texas are elected, giving rise to concerns about impartiality.

Jurisdiction in Texas

There are two basic types of law: **criminal law** and **civil law**. Criminal law has to do with crimes against the state. Though a victim is involved, the crime is viewed as occurring against the state, and thus the rights to pursue the defendant accrue to the state. Civil law, on the other hand, deals with non-criminal issues such as contracts, property law, family law, and tort law (or civil wrongs such as an injury resulting from maintaining a clearly dangerous situation in an area open to the public). Under civil law, the right to pursue a case accrues to the harmed individual rather than the state. This is a key distinction between criminal and civil law.

The right of a court to hear a case is known as **jurisdiction**. Courts are granted certain jurisdiction by the legislature or constitution. Reflective of the complexity of the Texas legal system, a single court can have jurisdiction over criminal matters, civil matters, or both. In addition to criminal and/ or civil jurisdiction, a court may have original and/or appellate jurisdiction. **Original jurisdiction** refers to a court's right to hear an initial case (these are trial courts). This case may include a jury. If a jury is included, the jury determines the facts (what happened) while the judge determines the law (how the law applies to what happened). Otherwise the judge determines issues of fact and law. **Appellate jurisdiction** refers to a court's right to hear an appeal from a trial court. Appellate cases do not include a jury, but rather include the judge as the finder of law (the facts are supposed to be accepted as determined by the trial court, though recent appellate courts in Texas have shown an increasing propensity for reinterpreting the facts as well). Certain courts have original jurisdiction in some instances and appellate jurisdiction in other instances. The same court can never have both original and appellate jurisdiction in a single case, however, because it would not make sense to appeal a court's decision to that very same court.[1]

Criminal Law

Criminal law denotes conduct that the state deems harmful to individuals, groups, or society itself. These acts are typically punishable by a fine, a jail sentence, or both. In the United States criminal law is usually divided into two categories: misdemeanors and felonies. Texas **misdemeanors** are further divided into three classes: A, B, or C. Class A misdemeanors are the most serious and can be punished by up to one year in jail and/or a fine of up to $4,000. Perjury is typically a class A misdemeanor, though Aggravated Perjury is a third degree felony.[22] Class B misdemeanors are the next most serious, and can be punished by up to 180 days in jail and/or a fine of up to $2,000. Possession of up to two ounces of marijuana is one example of a class B misdemeanor. Finally, class C misdemeanors are the least serious and typically involve only a fine of up to $500. Most Minor in Possession offenses are class C misdemeanors.[3] **Felonies** include first, second, third degree, and "state jail" felonies. First degree felonies are the most serious. These include crimes such as murder and sexual assault, or the theft of property of more than $200,000. First degree felonies are punishable by five to ninety-nine years in jail, a life sentence, or even a death sentence (in the case of a special type of first degree felony: the capital felony). Second degree felonies are less serious and include crimes such as aggravated assault or the theft of property between $100,000 and $200,000. These crimes are punishable by two to twenty years. Third degree felonies are less serious yet and include physical offenses not resulting in injury or theft of property valued between $20,000 and $100,000. **State jail felonies** are the least serious and include crimes such as credit card abuse or theft of property between $1,500 and $20,000, as well as certain drug offenses. They are punishable by 180 days to two years in jail.[4]

As noted above, some crimes can be punished by the death sentence. Since 1976 Texas leads the United States in executions. Nevertheless, though support for the death penalty is widespread in Texas, the number of executions has steadily trended downward. In 2014 ten people were executed in Texas, the lowest number in nearly two decades, though in 2015 thirteen were executed and as of October 25, 2016, seven had been executed. One reason for this trend is the inability of Texas to obtain the drugs used in capital punishment. Other reasons may include a US Supreme Court ruling banning the execution of the mentally disabled, another ruling banning the execution of those who were minors at the time of their crime, and the ability of Texas juries to now sentence murderers to life without parole. Crimes for which one may receive a death sentence include murdering during the commission of certain other felonies, murdering peace officers, and serial murder. These crimes are called **capital felonies**. Once a defendant is found guilty of a capital offense, three questions must be answered by the jury or judge (depending upon which is the finder of fact) to determine whether that person should suffer the death penalty. First, is the defendant a continuing threat to

---

1. Jones, Ericson, et al., *Practicing Texas Politics* (New York: Houghton Mifflin Company, 1998).

2. Texas Penal Code, Title 8. Offenses against Public Administration. Chapter 37. Perjury and Other Falsification. http://www.statutes.legis.state.tx.us/Docs/PE/htm/PE.37.htm#37.02.

3. Alcoholic Beverage Code. Title 4. Regulatory and Penal Provisions. Chapter 106. Provisions Relating to Age. http://www.statutes.legis.state.tx.us/Docs/AL/htm/AL.106.htm#106.071.

4. On punishments, see generally, Texas Penal Code, Title 3. Punishments. Chapter 12. Punishments. Subchapter A. General Provisions. http://www.statutes.legis.state.tx.us/Docs/PE/htm/PE.12.htm.

society? If not, the defendant may not be executed. Second, if the defendant was found guilty as a party to capital murder, did he or she intend or anticipate the killing? If both of these questions are answered in the affirmative, the finder of fact must next consider whether there is mitigating evidence from the defendant's background. Essentially, the finder of fact asks whether something in the defendant's background would reduce the defendant's culpability for the crime. If the answer to this question is yes, the defendant may not be executed. Thus, to execute someone in Texas, the finder of fact must decide the defendant remains a threat to society, that there are no mitigating circumstances in the defendant's background, and if the defendant was a party rather than a perpetrator, that he or she intended or anticipated the death of the victim. In the case of a jury, these decisions must be unanimous. If the finder of fact decides either that the defendant is no longer a threat to society or that there are mitigating circumstances in the defendant's background (or in the case of a party to the murder, that the murder was not intended or anticipated), the defendant is sentenced to life without a chance for parole instead of receiving the death penalty. If sentenced to death, the defendant has an automatic right of appeal to the Texas Court of Criminal Appeals, the highest criminal court in the state. Appeals are also allowed to federal courts. It has been estimated that it costs $2.3 million (some argue this number is inflated) to execute a defendant, while it costs about one-third of this to imprison a defendant for forty years.[5]

Civil Law

Civil law essentially refers to all law that is not criminal law. This includes things such as contract law, real property law, and tort law. Civil law typically concerns private parties, not the state. Most suits between private individuals and/or corporations fall under civil law. But a single event may lead to both criminal and civil cases. A discussion of civil law is far beyond the scope of this short primer. The interested student is encouraged to enroll in one of the courses at this university explicitly focused on civil law.

Courts in Texas

Courts in Texas can have exclusive jurisdiction or concurrent jurisdiction. **Exclusive jurisdiction** means that only one court may hear a case. **Concurrent jurisdiction** means that more than one court has a right to hear the same case (of course, only one court will ultimately hear the case). Where concurrent jurisdiction exists, the plaintiff chooses the court.

The most basic set of courts in Texas are local trial courts of limited jurisdiction. These courts include municipal courts and justice courts (formerly justice of the peace courts). **Municipal courts** are city courts. There are over 900 municipal courts in Texas.[6] They are trial courts only, and deal just with criminal matters having fines of less than $2,500 for violations of municipal ordinances or class C misdemeanors (criminal matters punishable by a fine of $500 or less with no jail time). The judges typically serve for two years and are appointed by city councils. Judge's qualifications are determined by the governing body of the city. Appeals from municipal court decisions go to county courts or district courts. Depending on the size and budget of the municipal court, they may or may

---

5. On the death penalty in Texas, see American Bar Association. 2013. Evaluating the Fairness and Accuracy in State Death Penalty Systems: The Texas Capital Punishment Assessment Report. American Bar Association. http://www.americanbar.org/content/dam/aba/administrative/death_penalty_moratorium/tx_complete_report.authcheckdam.pdf. See also, Jones, Ericson, et al., *Practicing Texas Politics*.
6. Ballotpedia, Texas Municipal Courts. https://ballotpedia.org/Texas_Municipal_Courts.

not have a record of the trial. If they have an official transcript of the trial, the appeal court will accept that record as determinative. If they have no official record (and most do not), then the county court will have an entirely new trial, called a **trial de novo**. Municipal judges also act as magistrates meaning they can issue warrants, determine bail, and undertake other judicial duties.[7]

Justice courts are precinct level courts. There are 817 justice courts spread across the counties of Texas. A Justice of the Peace (JP) is elected for a four-year term. Very few JP's are lawyers. Justice courts have original jurisdiction in certain civil and criminal matters. Exclusive civil jurisdiction is limited to matters of $200 or less (small claims court). These courts also have concurrent jurisdiction with county and district courts in civil matters between $200 and $10,000. Criminal matters are limited to those for which no jail time is possible. These courts are never courts of record hence any appeals to a county or district court will be trial de novo. JPs also have magistrate duties similar to those of a municipal court judge.[8]

The next level of courts in Texas is the county trial courts. These courts each have a single judge who is elected for a four-year term. There are actually three types of county trial courts in Texas: constitutional county courts, county courts at law, and probate courts. We will examine the constitutional county courts and the county courts at law.

Constitutional county courts have both original and appellate jurisdiction, as well as criminal and civil jurisdiction. Original civil jurisdiction is limited to amounts between $200 and $10,000. Criminal jurisdiction includes all misdemeanors with a fine of more than $500 or a jail sentence. The judges do not have to be licensed attorneys, but where they are not, any crime for which a defendant may have to serve jail time must be transferred to a district court at the request of either party. The appellate jurisdiction of these courts arises out of municipal courts and justice courts. Cases of original jurisdiction in the constitutional county court may be appealed to district courts.[9]

County courts of law were created by the legislature after the constitutional county courts. This system is continuously added to and modified by the legislature each time it meets. As you might imagine, this further complicates an already confusing system of justice in Texas. The judges in these courts are required to be attorneys. These courts typically handle misdemeanor criminal cases and civil disputes between $500 and $200,000, though jurisdiction can vary depending upon the particular statute by which the specific court was created.[10]

State district trial courts represent the next level of the Texas judicial system. The more than 450 district courts are the workhorses of trial courts in Texas. They are presided over by judges who have been elected to a four-year term. These judges must be licensed attorneys or have served as a judge for the previous four years. Vacant judgeships are filled by a governor's appointment. District courts typically accept both criminal and civil cases. Criminal jurisdiction is always original and concerns felony matters. Any capital felony (death penalty) conviction is immediately appealed to the Texas Court of Criminal Appeals, while other criminal convictions may be appealed to one of the courts of appeal. District trial courts have original civil jurisdiction over matters of $200 or more and therefore may have concurrent jurisdiction with certain lower courts.[11]

There are three sets of dedicated appellate courts in Texas. There are fourteen courts of appeal, one Texas Court of Criminal Appeals, and one Supreme Court of Texas. The fourteen **state courts**

---

7. See generally, Texas Courts: A Descriptive Summary, http://www.txcourts.gov/media/994672/Court-Overview.pdf.
8. See generally, Stefan Haag, Gary Keith, and Rex Peebles, *Texas Politics and Government.* (New York: Pearson Longman, 2003, 2005, 2012). See also, Texas Judicial Branch, About Texas Courts, http://www.txcourts.gov/courts/overview/about-texas-courts/trial-courts.aspx.
9. On constitutional county courts, see Texas Courts: A Descriptive Summary, http://www.txcourts.gov/media/10753/court-overview.pdf.
10. Texas Courts: A Descriptive Summary, http://www.txcourts.gov/media/10753/court-overview.pdf.
11. Ibid.

of appeal act as intermediate appellate courts for all courts of original jurisdiction. They accept all matters other than capital felonies. A further appeal from one of these courts of appeal may be made to the **Texas Court of Criminal Appeals** in the case of criminal matters or the **Supreme Court of Texas** in the case of civil matters. This makes Texas one of only two states in the United States that have two final appellate courts. Except in death penalty cases, all appeals to the Texas Court of Criminal Appeals or the Supreme Court of Texas are heard at the discretion of said court.[12]

All appellate courts in Texas have at least three judges, elected to six-year terms. Elections are staggered so that one-third of each court is up for re-election every two years. Appellate judges must be thirty-five years of age and have had ten years of experience as a practicing lawyer or judge. Vacancies on the court due to death, resignation, or removal are filled through appointment by the governor, with the advice and consent of the senate. All appellate level courts make their decisions by a majority vote.

Lawyers

Before becoming a lawyer one must gain entrance into law school. Though schools vary, typically admissions committees look at a student's Law School Admissions Test (LSAT) score, a student's grades, other factors such as letters of recommendation, ability to add diversity to a class, and extra-curricular activities. Law school is very expensive and should not be undertaken lightly. Though debt varies according to many factors, for the class of 2015 the average student debt for law school was over $118,889.[13] A prospective law student should decide what sort of law he or she wants to practice as early as possible. The sooner one decides the better one can take full advantage of the broad range of classes offered by most law schools. After law school, the student must pass the bar examination for the state in which he or she hopes to practice. Upon successfully completing the bar examination and passing a background check, the young lawyer is sworn in and entitled to practice law.

Lawyers are charged with aggressively representing their clients in an adversarial system. While there is a great deal of diversity in the sort of law one may practice, most lawyers either litigate (practice in court rooms) or engage in transactional law (prepare business deals). Subfields exist in each area. For example, a litigator could be a prosecutor, a criminal defense lawyer, a plaintiff's attorney, an insurance defense attorney, a white collar defense lawyer, a patent attorney, a commercial law attorney, or practice in any one of dozens of other litigation areas. Transactional practice areas include corporate, tax law, securities work, bank and finance, property law, and estate law. Some lawyers, such as patent attorneys, can be both litigators and transactional lawyers. Similarly, although the independent general practitioner still exists, many lawyers specialize today and work in some sort of firm. Increasingly, lawyers are employees rather than autonomous professionals. Also, lawyers tend to be concentrated in urban areas. Like the United States generally, there are many lawyers in Texas.

Juries

There are two types of juries in Texas: trial juries and grand juries. The **trial jury (or petit jury)** determines guilt or innocence in criminal trials, sometimes takes part in sentencing (in capital trials), and determines responsibility in civil trials. In civil cases where juries are an option, a jury may be

---

12. Ibid.
13. Federal Investment in Legal Education: Class of 2015, http://www.lawschooltransparency.com/reform/projects/Law-School-Financing/.

demanded by either party or waived by both. In a criminal case, the defendant can waive the right to a jury. In either case, when the jury is omitted the judge will determine facts as well as law. The trial jury is selected from a jury panel or venire, which itself is randomly chosen from a list of citizens. Though trial juries typically include twelve members, they sometimes can contain six. Very few trials involve juries, usually because of expense.[14]

A **grand jury** is made up of twelve citizens who sit on the jury for a number of months. Grand juries are intended to prevent abusive prosecutions by the state. Most grand juries sit for six months. Prosecutors bring information before the grand jury seeking an indictment. No defense presence is allowed before a grand jury. Consequently, though an indictment often seems very serious, in fact it simply demonstrates that an unchallenged prosecutor was able to convince the grand jury that a crime might have been committed. When indicted, a defendant must stand trial. If the grand jury fails to indict an individual (called a "no true bill"), the individual does not have to stand trial. Indictments are required only for felonies.[15]

Issues in the Texas Legal System

One issue in Texas revolves around whether we wish to advance accountability or independence in our judges. Accountability implies that we can punish judges who make decisions with which we disagree. Independence implies judges are not influenced by outside sources and are thus fairer. Texas has chosen to emphasize accountability over independence. We know this because most judges in Texas are elected and must stand for re-election on a regular basis. This means that a judge may be susceptible to external influences such as public opinion, partisanship, and special interests. Public opinion always is a factor in elections; moreover, judicial elections in Texas are partisan races and often the candidate's party is the only information available to the voter. In addition, a judge who must run for election requires money to finance his or her campaign. Much of this money will be donated. Judges can ask lawyers to donate money to the judge's campaign, even though this lawyer may later be involved in cases before the judge. This gives rise to a perception that those who donate significant sums of money to a judge's campaign may be favored in court. Even if this is not the case, judges are unlikely to make fair decisions when those decisions are exceptionally unpopular; instead, the judge may favor public opinion. Many Texans, lawyers, and even judges believe money influences legal decisions. One way to resolve this problem would be to adopt the **Missouri system** for judge selection. Here, the governor would appoint judges from a list presented by a committee of legal experts. After that judge has served some amount of time, he or she would be subject to a **retention election** whereby the voters decide whether to keep the judge. Another way to deal with the issue of judges fundraising for elections would be to bar judges from raising their own campaign money. In fact, Florida elects judges, but prohibits them from raising money for elections. The US Supreme Court upheld this rule in April 2015. Though a law was proposed in Texas to prohibit judges from campaign fundraising, this bill stalled. Indeed, although change has repeatedly been recommended and introduced in this area, the legislature has not passed any judicial selection reform.[16]

Tort reform has been another contentious issue in Texas. Some, such as doctors and business interests, have argued their vulnerability to lawsuits has made their insurance premiums prohibitively

---

14. Handbook of Texas Online, Joseph W. McKnight, "Jury Trial," accessed November 02, 2016, http://www.tshaonline.org/handbook/online/articles/jzj02.

15. Gary Halter, *Government and Politics of Texas*. (Boston, MA: McGraw Hill, 2005).

16. For this paragraph, see Haag, Keith, and Peebles, *Texas Politics and Government*. See also, Halter, *Government and Politics of Texas*.

high. Doctors have thus sought tort reform or limits to the amount of **punitive damages** one can recover in a medically related lawsuit (that is, damages intended to punish a wrongdoer in a civil action). Lawyers and consumer interest groups, on the other hand, have argued against limiting plaintiff recoveries, claiming a cap on damages will not lead to lower insurance premiums but will only increase doctor's salaries. The advocates of recovery limits placed a constitutional amendment proposal before Texans in 2003 (Proposition 12), which voters approved after an advertising campaign financed by doctors and the insurance industry. Individuals are now limited to a recovery of $250,000 in punitive damages against a medical professional in Texas courts—no matter how egregious the mistake. Typically additional damages are limited to lost wages, which some argue benefits the wealthy. Since lawyer's fees are often taken out of amounts recovered, the victim almost always ends up with less than $250,000.

Conclusion

The Texas judicial system is complex and beset by controversy. The complexity stems from an extremely decentralized court system. There are often multiple courts in which the same case may be heard. Sometimes a single court will have both original and appellate jurisdiction. In addition to its complexity, the Texas legal system has chosen to emphasize judicial accountability over independence. Judges are elected to office in Texas, injecting electoral politics into the judicial process. If judges hope to win office, they must make decisions that cater to public opinion. Further, they must collect large sums of money from lawyers and other interest groups in order to win elections, thereby raising the specter of favoritism. Finally, doctors (and some businesses) in Texas have managed to limit recovery for certain actions in tort. While this has reduced the number of lawsuits doctors are vulnerable to, it has also limited the ability of wronged patients to recover against doctors.

Key Terms

Criminal Law
Civil Law
Jurisdiction
Original Jurisdiction
Appellate Jurisdiction
Misdemeanor
Felony
Capital Felony
Exclusive Jurisdiction
Concurrent Jurisdiction
Municipal Court
Trial de novo
Justice of the Peace Court
Constitutional County Court
County Court of Law
State District Trial Court
State Courts of Appeal
Texas Court of Criminal Appeals
Supreme Court of Texas
Trial (Petit) Jury

References

Alcoholic Beverage Code. Title 4. Regulatory and Penal Provisions. Chapter 106. Provisions Relating to Age. http://www.statutes.legis.state.tx.us/Docs/AL/htm/AL.106.htm#106.071.

American Bar Association. 2013. Evaluating the Fairness and Accuracy in State Death Penalty Systems: The Texas Capital Punishment Assessment Report. American Bar Association. http://www.americanbar.org/content/dam/aba/administrative/death_penalty_moratorium/tx_complete_report.authcheckdam.pdf

Beck, Paul and Frank Sorauf. 1992. *Party Politics in America.* New York: HarperCollins.

Death Penalty Information Center: Facts about the Death Penalty. 19 October 2016. http://www.deathpenaltyinfo.org/documents/FactSheet.pdf.

Ford, Matt. 2014. "In Texas, the Death Penalty is Slowly Dying Out." *The Atlantic.* http://www.theatlantic.com/national/archive/2014/10/texas-death-penalty-executions/382057/

Haag, Stefan, Gary Keith, and Rex Peebles. 2003, 2005, 2012. *Texas Politics and Government.* New York: Pearson Longman.

Halter, Gary. 2005. *Government and Politics of Texas.* Boston, MA: McGraw Hill.

Jones, Ericson, et al. 1998. *Practicing Texas Politics.* New York: Houghton Mifflin Company.

Maxwell, William, Ernest Crain, et al. 2006. *Texas Politics Today.* Belmont, CA: Thomson Wadsworth.

Ramsey, Ross. 2015. "Analysis: Should Judges Exit Fundraising Business." *Texas Tribune.* http://www.texastribune.org/2015/05/15/analysis-distance-between-judges-and-politics/

St. John, Debra. 2004. *Texas Politics Supplement.* New York: Pearson Longman

Texas Penal Code, Title 3. Punishments. Chapter 12. Punishments. Subchapter A. General Provisions. http://www.statutes.legis.state.tx.us/Docs/PE/htm/PE.12.htm.

Texas Penal Code, Title 8. Offenses against Public Administration. Chapter 37. Perjury and Other Falsification. http://www.statutes.legis.state.tx.us/Docs/PE/htm/PE.37.htm#37.02.

Todd, John. 1999. *Texas Politics: The Challenge of Change.* New York: Houghton Mifflin.

Exercise 4.1 ■ Multiple Choice

1. The Texas legal system:
   a. includes only civil matters.
   b. is a centralized hierarchy.
   c. is exceptionally complex.
   d. is tightly interwoven with the federal system such that federal and state judges can both hear the same cases.

2. The two basic types of law in Texas are:
   a. civil and commercial.
   b. civil and criminal.
   c. criminal and commercial.
   d. trial and appellate.

3. In Texas courts, jurisdiction can be:
   a. civil only.
   b. trial only.
   c. appellate only.
   d. criminal, civil, or both.

4. Original jurisdiction refers to:
   a. the right to hear a matter initially or in the first instance.
   b. the right to hear a matter on appeal.
   c. the right to hear cases in district courts only.
   d. the right to hear criminal matters.

5. Which of the following is the most serious type of felony?
   a. Class A
   b. First degree
   c. Second degree
   d. Third degree

6. A defendant who is found guilty of a capital felony in Texas may only be executed if the jury finds:
   a. there are no mitigating circumstances for the defendant.
   b. the defendant has no mitigating circumstances but does not represent a continuing threat to the public.
   c. the defendant has mitigating circumstances, but presents a threat to the public.
   d. the defendant continues to represent a threat to the public and has no mitigating circumstances.

7. Concurrent jurisdiction means that:
   a.   two courts may hear the same type of matter.
   b.   two courts may hear the same matter at the same time.
   c.   only trial courts may hear the matter.
   d.   criminal and civil courts may both hear the matter.

8. Which courts may only hear criminal matters?
   a.   Justice of the peace courts
   b.   Municipal courts
   c.   District courts
   d.   The Supreme Court of Texas

9. Which jury hears matters in which no defense presence is allowed?
   a.   Petit juries
   b.   Trial juries
   c.   Grand juries
   d.   Special juries

10. Texas emphasizes which of the following concepts for its judges?
   a.   Accountability
   b.   Impartiality
   c.   Impartiality and accountability
   d.   Neither impartiality nor accountability

Exercise 4.2 ■ Research Exercise

Write a short essay explaining why tort reform has been sought in Texas. Find and summarize at least one Internet article discussing the results of such reform.

Exercise 4.3 ■ Analytical Essay—Functions of Courts

What are the main courts of Texas? What are their respective responsibilities?

Exercise 4.4 ■ Analytical Essay—Judicial Selection

Discuss the difference between accountability and impartiality for Texas judges. Which has Texas decided to emphasize and with what result?

CHAPTER 5

Local Government in Texas

Dr. Alan I. Baily

I. Local Government Yesterday and Today

Today, few citizens pay attention to the activities of local government. Print and broadcast media generally keep the public informed of politics at the national level. Most of the hot-button issues are debated in the national or state legislatures. As a consequence of these and other changes, it is rare for Americans today to think much about local government, in spite of the fact that it's the level of government that is closest to our own lives.

Of course, this was not always the case. Indeed, in Colonial and Early Republican America, citizens of many regions of the country were robust participants in local democracy. Perhaps the most famous example of this was the New England Town-Hall meeting. In 1813, Thomas Jefferson, a Virginian, expressed admiration for the New England tradition of "town-hall" government in a letter to John Adams, of Massachusetts. In the same letter, Jefferson sketched his (unrealized) plan for a public school system in Virginia that would have relied on similarly small units of local government, called "wards." Jefferson's wards would bear responsibility not only for administering the schools, but also for "the care of their poor, their roads, police, elections, the nomination of jurors, administration of justice in small cases, [and] elementary exercises of militia." As Jefferson envisioned them, the wards would be "little republics . . . for all those concerns which, being under their eye, they would better manage than the larger republics of the county or State."[1]

Jefferson admired such small local institutions not only because he believed that some public goods are managed better at the local level, as opposed to the State or National level, but also because

---

1. Thomas Jefferson to John Adams (1813). In Isaac Kramnick and Theodore J. Lowi, eds., *American Political Thought* (New York: Norton, 2009), 368.

he believed direct participation in local politics would educate average citizens to wield political authority in a responsible way—an important skill for the citizens of a newborn democratic republic.

Echoing Jefferson's opinion, Alexis de Tocqueville, a French observer of the young democracy, stressed the importance of Americans' robust participation in civic and political associations. Tocqueville, too, saw participation in voluntary local associations as an essential aspect of democratic citizenship. The Americans' habits of association, Tocqueville believed, arose from crucial differences between the (American) democratic citizen's way of life and the lives of monarchical or aristocratic (European) subjects. He wrote:

> Aristocratic societies always include within them, in the midst of a multitude of individuals who can do nothing by themselves, a few very powerful and very wealthy citizens; each of these can execute great undertakings by himself . . .

> In democratic peoples, on the contrary, all citizens are independent and weak; they can do almost nothing by themselves, and none of them can oblige those like themselves to lend them their cooperation. They therefore all fall into impotence if they do not learn to aid each other freely.

> If men who live in democratic countries had neither the right nor the taste to unite in political goals, their independence would run great risks, but they could preserve their wealth and their enlightenment for a long time; whereas if they did not acquire the practice of associating with each other in ordinary life, civilization itself would be in peril.[2]

Local Government Today

Local government has always made a greater impact on the average citizen's daily life than either state or national government; but this is especially true today. In the twenty-first century, local governments manage a vast array of public goods that affect the quality of people's everyday lives. Generally speaking, the institutions and agencies of local government are far more complex today than they were in the nineteenth, or even the early twentieth century.

The same cannot be said of political participation at the local level. Most citizens today are not too interested in local government. The majority of the goods and services that local governments administer—such as clean water, paved roads, public schools, waste management, and the protection of life and property—are public goods that we tend to take for granted. Public goods like these are non-controversial; for the most part, citizens agree on their value and rarely grouse about having to pay taxes for their upkeep. Moreover, since the management of these goods has largely been turned over to professional administrators, average citizens experience both a lack of opportunity, and of motivation, to participate in governance at the local level.

Of the many changes to local life that have transpired over the last couple of centuries, two in particular can help explain the distinct character of local government and politics today. The first is the professionalization of public administration, which arose during the progressive era. The second is the gradual nationalization, and present-day globalization, of the commercial economy. Both of these developments have altered the landscape of local politics significantly.

The rise of professional administration was fueled by progressive-era reformers' conviction that local governments (especially the large urban "machines") were dominated by partisan cronies more

---

2. Alexis de Tocqueville, *Democracy in America.* Translated by Harvey Mansfield and Delba Winthrop.

interested in securing their own power than the public good. Reformers put their confidence in a new class of professionally trained managers, whom they believed would be more effective stewards of public goods. Today, the daily operations of medium and large-sized cities are managed not by elected officials, but by professional administrators who are appointed by the city's elected leaders. The virtues of professional management include expertise, competence, and autonomy from partisan political pressures. At best, professionalization has increased the competence of local administration, but at the cost of democratic accountability through elections.

The second, no less important, change in the nature of local government is related to the vast enlargement of the spheres of production and exchange. Before the rise of mechanized industry and the corporation, virtually all the necessities of life, and even many luxury goods, were produced in the local community. Today's global economy is more far-flung; most of the basic consumer goods we enjoy come from faraway places, and economic elites (as well as workers) tend to be very mobile, rather than rooted in one local community.

In past times, political and economic elite groups tended to overlap at the local level, and these political-economic elites exercised the preponderance of influence in the local community. But today, local government elites have more autonomy from business and economic elites. There is an obvious benefit to this new arrangement, as it enables local government to deliver public goods and services free of undue interference from private interests. However, one downside of this situation is that it discourages upwardly-mobile businesspeople from enlisting their organizational and leadership abilities in public service.

Urbanization

Another important change deserves mention here, but it applies mainly to urban communities. One hundred years ago, approximately 80 percent of Texans lived in the rural countryside. At that time, the countryside was the site of most economic production, since Texas's wealth relied on farming, ranching, and natural resources. The second half of the twentieth century saw a marked diversification in Texas's economy, and the majority of this economic growth took place in the cities. Today, land and natural resources are supplemented by industry, high technology, banking, finance, service, education, research, and more, as sources of the state's wealth. The enormous expansion of the urban economy in Texas has shifted much of the state's population into the cities. Today more than 80 percent of Texans live in urban areas, and less than 20 percent in the countryside.

The ballooning population of Texas's major cities has made the work of urban municipalities more complex. As a result, city governments in urban areas have become more complex and more active than smaller, rural municipalities. One register of this divergence is Texans' differing perceptions of the role of *county* government. Many urbanites today see county government as a redundancy, since the cities provide many services that the county provides, usually more extensively, and with greater efficiency. But county government has a more visible presence and a more significant role to play in rural areas, where municipal (city) governments are small and underfunded, if existent.

A final consequence of urbanization that deserves our attention is *suburbanization*. As the metropolitan population has swelled beyond city limits, and as, in some cases, wealthier residents have fled deteriorating inner cities; the number of small and autonomous municipalities on the outskirts of major cities has multiplied. These "suburbs" rely on the metropolitan economy for their existence, yet they contain tax revenue and other mobile resources within their own political boundaries. The suburbanization trend may have slowed lately, but it is not likely to reverse. While suburbanization has been popular, critics often point to resource inequalities and the neglect of historic urban communities as its negative externalities

II. Local Government Powers and Institutions

Dillon's Rule: Local Government's (Lack of) Legal Autonomy

In the US constitutional and federal system, the national government has only limited authority over the states. But in most cases, the same relationship does *not* subsist *within* states. The US Constitution is silent regarding the powers of local governments. As a result many state constitutions classify local governments as "creatures of the state."

This legal principle is called **Dillon's Rule** (it was formulated by Missouri Judge John Marshall Dillon in 1868). According to Dillon's Rule, "Municipal corporations owe their origin to, and derive their powers and rights wholly from, the legislature. It breathes into them the breath of life, without which they cannot exist. As it creates, so may it destroy. If it may destroy, it may abridge and control."[3]

In plain language, Dillon's Rule denies to local government the right of self-determination that both national and state governments enjoy. Thirty-nine of the fifty states, including Texas, enshrine Dillon's Rule in some form. Accordingly, in spite of the fact that local governments often have a great degree of *political* autonomy, they have very little *legal* authority; and whatever authority they have is subject to the will of the state's government.

The Texas Marriage Amendment supplies a good example of the effect of Dillon's Rule. This amendment stipulated (1) that marriage in Texas is heterosexual; and (2) that neither the state nor any local government may create or recognize any legal equivalent of marriage that does not meet the above definition. So, even if a local government wished to recognize a gay marriage or civil union that originated in another state (let alone create one), it would be prohibited by state law from doing so. Recent developments at the federal level have challenged the state's marriage amendment in significant respects, but local governments remain powerless to affect the issue.

Another more recent example of state government sovereignty over local governments in Texas is the legislative repeal of Denton's 2014 ban on hydraulic fracturing, or "fracking." Fracking is a new method of seeking and extracting fossil fuels that has generated some controversy as its environmental impacts are not well understood. In a November 2014 election nearly 59 percent of Denton voters approved a local ban on fracking. However, when the state legislature met the following spring, Texas representatives passed House Bill 40. The measure prohibits local governments from restricting oil and gas exploration. Governor Abbot signed the bill and fracking returned to Denton in the summer of 2015.

In the 2017 session the Texas Legislature will consider a measure to overturn "bag ban" policies, which were adopted by the cities of Laredo and Austin. These policies do not literally ban plastic bags, but the city assesses a charge for each plastic bag a consumer uses (e.g., at grocery stores). Governor Abbot has also endorsed a policy to strip state funds from so-called "sanctuary cities." There is no formal legal definition of a "sanctuary city" but the term refers to municipalities that do not punish unauthorized immigrants for violating federal immigration laws. For better or worse, the Texas Legislature continues to scrutinize local policies, and occasionally, restrict municipalities' authority under state law.

---

3. Clinton v Cedar Rapids and the Missouri River Railroad, 24 Iowa 455; 1868.

Types of Local Government

There are three main types of local government in Texas: cities (or municipalities), counties, and special districts. A **city** is a **general purpose government**, which means that a city has the general power of legislation—in any matter where state or federal law is silent, city government is free to act. Municipal laws are called **ordinances**. Ordinances are municipal government's equivalent to the statutes passed by legislatures.

Both **counties** and **special districts** are **special purpose**, or limited purpose, local governments. Special purpose governments are governmental institutions designed for a specific purpose, and empowered to regulate affairs in that area alone. Limited purpose governments lack the general power of legislation.

The Texas Constitution specifies that all county governments in Texas shall have the same governmental structure and perform the same, limited functions. Counties serve the state government in a variety of administrative functions defined by the Texas Constitution. These functions include the maintenance of county roads, record-keeping, and law enforcement.

A special district is a limited purpose local government that fulfills one specific role. Basically, special districts exercise a great degree of authority within a single, narrowly-defined, jurisdiction. The most common example of a special district is a school district, which exercises almost exclusive authority over the administration of public schools within a given territory. Other examples of special purpose government include transit districts, utility districts, and sports authorities.

City Government

The basis of a city's legal authority is the city **charter**. A city's charter is akin to a constitution; it spells out the basic rights and powers, and the structure, of municipal government. In Texas, a municipality is either a **general law** city, or a **home rule** city. A general law city must adopt its charter from a list of approved models specified in the Texas Constitution. In contrast, a home rule city may write its own charter, so long as it does not include anything that violates state (or federal) law. General law cities have very narrow powers, in addition to having little flexibility regarding their basic form of government. By state law, any municipality with a population under 5,000 must be a general law city. Cities with a population greater than 5,000 have the option of becoming home rule cities, if the residents vote to do so. Most cities large enough to do so choose home rule because of the greater discretion it offers to municipal government.

Municipal Elections and Forms of City Government

Municipal Elections and Politics

In any representative democracy, the primary way that citizens keep officials accountable is by regularly scheduled, free, and competitive elections. This goes for city government as well. However, the manner of electing officials at the local level often differs from state and federal elections. For one thing, most municipal elections are **nonpartisan**, in the sense that candidates do not run on a political party's ticket and no party affiliation is published on the ballot. Nevertheless, coalitions often form in city politics (particularly in large cities) that play much the same role as political parties.

Another distinguishing feature involves the form of municipal elections. Many municipalities employ **at-large** elections for city council, rather than using **single-member districts**. In an at-large election, every eligible voter in the city may cast a ballot for every seat up for grabs on the council. In other words, seats on the council are *not* divided among different precincts of the city, with each precinct electing one councilor; instead, every resident votes in every contest. At-large elections can produce very disproportionate results, since the bloc of voters with the highest turnout is likely to win all of the seats. For this reason, many medium- and large-sized cities have transitioned from at-large elections to single-member districts (including Dallas, Houston, San Antonio and Nacogdoches—but, surprisingly, not Austin). Many city councils combine at-large seats and single-member districts.

Municipal politics can take many different shapes, depending on factors ranging from the size and demographic makeup of the city, to the city's electoral institutions. In large and complex cities the development of stable political coalitions and the use of single-member districts can produce a politics that resembles state and national electoral contests. In smaller and less diverse municipalities, a **friends-and-neighbors** style of politics tends to prevail, in which the candidate(s) who can turn out the greatest number of personal supporters wins the (typically little-attended) election.

Forms of City Government

Just as at other levels of government, municipal institutions exercise legislative, executive and judicial powers. The different forms of city government reflect different ways of dividing legislative, executive, and judicial authority. Since all municipal judges in Texas are appointed, the following discussion will focus on the different ways of distributing legislative and executive power in cities.

The most common form of city government—both in Texas, and nationally—is the **council-manager** form. In council-manager systems, an elected city council wields legislative power, while executive power is exercised by a professional city manager. The city manager is appointed (and may be removed) by the council. The mayor of the city is a member of the city council, who is chosen by council to preside over meetings, something like a chairperson. In council-manager systems the mayor is *primus inter pares*, or "first among equals." In other words, the mayor does not possess any formal executive authority; however, mayors may exercise some informal power over city government, particularly through agenda-setting.

The proliferation of the council-manager form of government reflects the growing complexity of municipal administration, as well as the increasing popularity of professional, rather than amateur, public management. In this system, being a city councilor, or even mayor, is a part-time job. Except in large cities, members of council are not paid and receive no staff support. But city managers and other municipal administrators are full-time salaried professionals with specialized training. As mentioned above, one drawback to this system is that appointed public administrators are not directly accountable to voters. But the city manager is accountable to the council, and so is accountable to voters, in an indirect way.

Some cities employ the **strong mayor-council** form of government. In this form, the mayor is a separately-elected official with executive authority, and is politically independent from the council. The council may be elected at-large, or by single-member districts, but the mayor's office is elected separately by the city as a whole. This form of government is popular in larger cities where political dynamics tend to be more complex, and the mayor is a more high-profile office. These cities, too, rely on many professional administrators to manage municipal affairs, but the appointment (and removal) power rests with the mayor rather than the council.

The **weak mayor-council** form also includes a separate mayor's office. However, in this system the mayor has very little executive power. The mayor may preside over the council, but in many cases, the mayor does not have the right to vote, except to break a tie.

Finally, the **commission** form of government was quite common in Texas at one time, though it is not very popular today. In this system, each member of the city council (or commission) is a separately elected executive official who plays a double role as a legislative official. Citizens might elect a police commissioner, fire commissioner, tax commissioner, and so on—and together these commissioners would comprise the council, in addition to administering their respective departments in an executive capacity. The commission system may be the most democratic form of municipal government since both executive and legislative power is subject directly to the power of voters. The drawback of this system is its amateurism: The commission system does not emphasize competence in the administration of public affairs. For example, one might be elected fire commissioner without having had any experience in firefighting—the only qualification for the job is electability.

County Government in Texas

By constitutional mandate, all 254 **counties** in Texas have the same (limited) purposes and the same structure. The purposes of county government include record-keeping (birth and death certificates), taxation, road maintenance, and law enforcement. In structure, county governments in Texas resemble the commission system described above. This is not surprising, since the form of county government is prescribed by the 1876 constitution and that document, generally speaking, provides for an amateur government. The framers of the Texas Constitution feared professional politicians and structure of both state and county government reflects their concerns.

County officials (including judges) are elected in **partisan** races. Also, unlike most municipal officials, county officials receive a salary and may receive staff support. The main governing body at the county level is the **county commissioner's court**, which consists of four **commissioners** elected in separate precincts and one **county judge**, elected by the entire county. Each of these officials serves a four-year term. It is best to think of the commissioner's court as an executive rather than a legislative or judicial body. Titles like "county judge" or "commissioner's court," can be misleading, since these officials perform judicial functions rarely, if ever. The commissioner's court is not empowered to write ordinances, but it does have the authority to approve the county budget, set the property tax rate (within prescribed limits), maintain county roads, and enforce state law within its jurisdiction. Also, the commissioner's court exercises limited appointment power.

Texas counties have a **plural executive** structure, with a host of countywide elected officials exercising authority alongside the county judge and commissioner's court. These officials include the county comptroller, county attorney, tax collector-appraiser, county clerk, and the county sheriff. Each of these officials receives a salary and staff support.

As mentioned above, particularly in urban areas, much of the work of county government seems redundant. Highly developed municipal governments already perform many of the same functions as county government. By contrast, in rural areas the county's role—in law enforcement and road maintenance, especially—is more valued. Unfortunately, it is difficult to address these different perceptions of the value of county government by scaling down counties in urban areas. The purposes and form of counties is written into the state constitution, so it would require a change to the constitution to effect a change in county governments' role.

Special Districts

Special districts are limited-purpose local governments which exercise a great deal of authority over a narrowly-defined jurisdiction. School districts, transit districts, utility districts, hospital districts, and sports authorities are all examples of special districts. Like other local governments, special districts typically are overseen by elected officials who serve part-time and administered by full-time appointed professionals. For example, voters elect members of a local school board, and that board, in turn, will appoint a superintendent and other administrators to manage the school district. In this way administrators are indirectly accountable to voters.

A special district's jurisdiction may cross over city or county lines. For example, the Municipal Utility District delivers utilities within Houston city limits but it also has jurisdiction over unincorporated areas in the vicinity of Houston; the Carrollton-Farmer's Branch ISD has jurisdiction over public schools in both Carrolton and Farmer's Branch (two suburbs of Dallas); and the Dallas Area Rapid Transit district (DART) oversees public transportation in Dallas and many of the surrounding suburbs. This overlapping jurisdiction requires formal agreements among municipal governments. Each participating government must consent to allow the special district's jurisdiction and to share the tax burden for whatever service the special district provides. The Dallas suburbs of Mesquite, Terrell, and Forney have not consented to DART's jurisdiction, for example—although they are reconsidering this at present.[4] In 2012, the city of Mesquite opened its first DART service, though it has not joined the DART system.

Local Government Revenue in Texas

Where do local governments get most of their funding? The main source of local government revenue is the property tax. Property tax is assessed by county government and tax revenues are divided among the various local governments that serve a particular area. For example, the main source of funding for a public school district is local property taxes—not state or federal funds. In addition to property tax, municipal governments are authorized to assess a sales tax of up to 2 percent. (Most sales tax revenue enters the state's coffers; the state sales tax rate is 6.25 percent.)

Because Texas is a low-tax and low-spending state, much of the burden for financing local public goods falls directly on local property taxes. There is little state money to supplement local governments. The outside aid local governments do receive typically flows from federal revenue. The result of this arrangement has been a steady increase in Texans' property tax burden. Many critics, including the State Supreme Court, have challenged this tax-shifting arrangement, but despite widespread criticism the Texas legislature has not devised a way to ease the burden on local governments, primarily because doing so would require increasing revenue (i.e., increasing taxes) at the state level. Obviously, this would be a politically unpopular move.

Key Terms

General-law City	Strong Mayor-Council Form
Home-rule City	Council-Manager Form
At-large Election	Commission Form
Single-member District	Commissioners Court
Nonpartisanship	Plural Executive (in Counties)
Friends-and-neighbors Politics	General-purpose Government
Ordinance	Limited/Single-purpose Government
Weak Mayor-Council Form	

---

4. Terrell Mesquite and Forney ask DART to Explore Service. *The Dallas Morning News*, September 12, 2008.

References

Clinton v Cedar Rapids and the Missouri River Railroad, 24 Iowa 455; 1868.

Dahl, Robert. 1961. *WHO GOVERNS? Democracy and Power in an American City.* New Haven and London: Yale University Press.

Kramnick, Isaac and Theodore J. Lowi, eds. 2009. *American Political Thought.* New York: Norton.

The Texas Constitution. Available online at: http://www.statutes.legis.state.tx.us/.

Exercise 5.1 ■ Multiple Choice

1. In Texas,
    a. there is little land for new development
    b. rural areas are growing faster than in urban areas
    c. there is virtually no growth from decade to decade
    d. urban areas are growing faster than rural areas

2. The pluralistic perspective says
    a. cities are composed of many different ethnic/racial groups
    b. city government governs pluralistically
    c. informal power rests in different groups
    d. there is a power elite in cities

3. The main source of revenue for local government is
    a. sales tax
    b. property tax
    c. income tax
    d. luxury tax

4. Special districts
    a. are illegal in Texas
    b. use the commission form of government
    c. answer to cities
    d. operate independently from cities and counties

5. Typically, city council members
    a. are powerful
    b. are amateurs, part-time city officials
    c. are salaried
    d. officially meet on a daily basis

6. The US Constitution
    a. makes provisions for home-rule charters
    b. is silent concerning local governments
    c. places great restrictions on cities
    d. prevents states from creating cities

7. Typically, municipal elections are
    a. partisan
    b. independent
    c. nonpartisan
    d. informal

8. Which if the following is *not* an example of a special district?
   a. independent school district
   b. transit district
   c. police department
   d. hospital district

9. The city manager
   a. is elected
   b. is part-time
   c. executes council decisions
   d. is appointed by the mayor or council

10. All counties in Texas
    a. are equally populated
    b. have a county manager
    c. have ordinance making power
    d. have the same governing structure

Exercise 5.2 ■ Research Exercise

Visit the website of the Texas Legislature. Find a new law passed in the latest legislative session which deals with cities or counties. Make a copy of that law and attach it to this page.

Exercise 5.3   ■   Internet Research Exercise

Answer the following. What city in Texas is your hometown? What form of city government does it have? From that city's webpage, list three powers of the city council or the city manager. Also provide the address of the webpage you visited.

Exercise 5.4 ■ Field Research Exercise

Attend a city council meeting or meeting of the county commissioner's court. Obtain a copy of the agenda for the meeting. Attach the agenda to this sheet. Stay at the meeting for at least one hour. What decision(s) did they make while you were there?

CHAPTER 6

An Exploration of Texas Public Policy

Dr. Cindy Davis

Public policy involves what government does and how it does it. The state of Texas is active in multiple policy arenas and here we examine a select number of them. This chapter addresses several substantive areas of public policy including fiscal policy, education policy, social welfare policy, environmental policy, and energy policy. Government is involved in establishing and implementing these various policy areas, each of which has a substantial impact on the citizens of the state ranging from how the state chooses to collect your taxpayer dollars to how the state keeps the air clean for its citizens.

Fiscal Policy

One of the most essential areas of public policy for any level of government is fiscal policy, meaning the way government collects revenue and spends that revenue. **Fiscal policy** is the area of government policy focused on taxing and spending, basically the budgetary concerns of policy. The budget is a primary document that reveals fiscal policy. While students often find this a dry area of study, it is important to understand how the state collects its revenues and how the state uses the revenue it collects. This is because fiscal policy reflects the priorities of the state and which agencies and programs the state chooses to spend taxpayer (your) dollars on.

In general, the state of Texas is considered a low tax state meaning in comparison to other states tax rates are relatively low. Unlike the federal government which relies primarily on the individual income tax for revenue, the state of Texas does not have a state income tax. Instead, Texas relies on the general sales tax, established in 1961, as a primary source of revenue. The state has a set sales tax rate on the majority of goods at 6.25 percent. The estimated revenue for the 2016–2017 biennium from sales taxes is 28 percent of total revenue which is the second highest estimated revenue source behind federal funds estimated to bring in 34 percent of the total revenue stream.[1]

The 1967 Local Sales and Use Tax Act allows local governments to add to this sales tax rate and mass transit authorities and special districts may also have the option of adding to the sales tax. However, no more than 2 percent total may be added to the 6.25 percent general sales tax rate. As a result, the sales tax rate may effectively total up to 8.25 percent. Originally there were restrictions on how the additional city sales tax could be formulated, but with the passage of House Bill 157 which was signed into law by Governor Greg Abbott in 2015 local governments were given additional flexibility in determining whether to increase or decrease the amount by holding elections, so long as the amount does not exceed the 2 percent total cap. This bill is seen as a mechanism for local governments to develop more flexible fiscal policies to aid their particular areas.

The sales tax is considered a **regressive tax**. This means the higher your tax base is, the lower your tax rate is. To put it in terms of income, a person with a higher income (base) will pay less of a percentage of their income (rate) in overall sales tax. A regressive tax is seen to impact those at lower income levels more drastically than those at higher income levels. This is in contrast to a **progressive tax** (such as an income tax) where the tax rate increases as the tax base increases, meaning for example that a higher income would be taxed at a higher rate. A progressive tax is seen as impacting the wealthier more than the poor with one rationale behind progressive taxes as based on the idea that those with the ability to pay more should pay more. Fiscal policy in Texas is considered to be based on a more regressive tax system than a progressive tax system.

The state collects a number of other taxes and has other streams of revenue in addition to the general sales tax. These include specific taxes on sales of motor vehicles, "sin" taxes on goods such as alcohol and cigarettes and severance taxes on the production of oil and gas. The severance tax, while once a large percentage of state revenue has dropped and the estimated collection for severance taxes for 2016–2017 was only 2.7 percent of total state revenue[2]. Other streams of revenue come from the federal government such as in the form of grants-in-aid, and from sources such as lottery funds, licensing, and returns on investment. A specific revenue fund to be aware of is the **Economic Stabilization Fund** (ESF), also known as the "Rainy Day Fund" which became effective in 1989 after being adopted as part of the Texas Constitution in 1988. The fund receives revenue from severance taxes, surplus funds left over from the general fund at the end of the biennium budget cycle, interest on the fund, and any direct appropriations the Legislature chooses to make to the fund. This particular revenue fund is only to be used in times of financial emergency such as when there are budget deficits, revenue shortfalls, or for purposes deemed necessary by the Legislature. Examples of uses of the ESF include disaster relief and economic development needs. At the end of the 2016 fiscal year the amount in the ESF was estimated to be around $9.7 billion, the largest rainy day fund in the nation that year. Maintaining a strong ESF can be a sound fiscal policy for Texas but note that it can lead to heated debates during legislative sessions when the state is facing budgetary challenges in regard to whether the fund should be tapped and, if so, by how much.

For local governments, the primary source of revenue is the property tax which is an ad valorem tax based on the appraisal of property. The tax rate is set by the local government. While taxes collected by the state of Texas are considered low, local taxes are considered relatively high.

State spending is reflected in the state budget which is passed every two years during the legislative session. Spending by the state has been increasing as the population of Texas increases. Along with this, of course, comes the fact that there will be more individuals contributing revenue to the

---

1. Legislative Budget Board, "Fiscal Size-Up 2016–2017 Biennium," May 2016, http://www.lbb.state.tx.us/Documents/Publications/Fiscal_SizeUp/Fiscal_SizeUp.pdf.
2. Ibid.

state. Texas has one of the largest budgets in the nation, behind only California and New York as of 2014.[3] For the 2016–2017 biennium, the largest categories of budgetary expenditures from the general revenue funds were education, health and human services, and public safety and criminal justice.[4]

The Texas Constitution places a number of restrictions on the state budget. For example, as found in Article III Section 49a of the Texas Constitution, the state must operate on a pay-as-you-go system meaning the state must create a balanced budget. State borrowing and debt is kept at a minimum. Another example of a constitutional restriction on the budget is that the state cannot appropriate more than 1 percent of the budget to welfare programs for needy families and children under programs such as Temporary Assistance to Needy Families.

While the Texas Legislature passes the budget, two other actors have a powerful role in determining fiscal policy in the state. The first is the **Comptroller of Public Accounts** who is required to determine and certify what the expected revenues will be for the next budget cycle and who must approve appropriations of the legislature to ensure they meet within the spending guidelines. The other important actor is the **Legislative Budget Board** (LBB). The LBB was established in 1949 and oversees and coordinates the state budget process. The LBB creates the initial budget estimates for sessions of the Texas Legislature and creates fiscal policy notes for each bill.

Education Policy

Many students are aware of the way in which education policy can impact them such as what types of standardized tests they are required to take during high school to how much the cost of tuition will increase over the next few years. This section begins with an examination of elementary and secondary education policy and then turns to a discussion of higher education policy in Texas.

Texas has been active in elementary and secondary education policy for some time. In 1915 the state passed a compulsory attendance law and in 1918 an amendment was added to the Texas Constitution providing for free textbooks. However, it was not until the passage of the 1949 Gilmer-Aikin Act that really pushed education policy by guaranteeing public education for twelve years with a minimum of 175 days of schooling each year and established the Texas Education Agency. In 1981 the Texas Legislature established a statewide curriculum and in 1984, under the Education Reform Act, standardized testing for students and teacher competency testing were implemented.

There are a range of actors involved in establishing policy at this level. The State Board of Education is an elected fifteen-member board and is involved in policy issues such as curriculum, textbook adoption and oversees the Permanent School Fund. The **Texas Education Agency** (TEA) is the main agency that governs the elementary and secondary public education system. Its responsibilities include the distribution of funding to schools, providing support to the State Board of Education in areas such as curriculum development and monitoring compliance with state and federal guidelines. The TEA is supervised by the Commissioner of Education who is appointed by the governor. An important policy overseen by the TEA is assessment and testing specifically of the State of Texas Assessments of Academic Readiness (STAAR) exams which were implemented in 2012 and succeeded the Texas Assessment of Knowledge and Skills (TAKS) testing program. STAAR requires annual testing for various subjects at different grade levels and end-of-course testing in areas such

3. Kaiser Family Foundation, "State Health Facts: Total State Expenditures (in millions)," 2016, http://kff.org/other/state-indicator/total-state-spending/?currentTimeframe=0&sortModel=%7B%22colId%22:%22Total%20State%20Expenditures%20(in%20millions)%22,%22sort%22:%22desc%22%7D.

4. Legislative Budget Board, "Summary of Appropriations for the 2016–2017 Biennium," February, 2016, http://www.lbb.state.tx.us/Documents/Budget/Session_Code_84/2580_84_BillSummary.pdf.

as English, Algebra, US history, and biology. While assessment and testing of elementary and secondary students continues to provide for heated debate, it is unlikely to be done away with completely but instead the manner in which assessment and testing is implemented is a regularly disputed policy in elementary and secondary education.

One of the most contentious policy issues facing elementary and secondary schools has to do with how education is funded. Education is funded at the federal, state, and local levels, but the state and local levels provide the bulk of the funding. In 1854 Texas established the Permanent School Fund that today is combined with a portion of the motor fuels tax to create the Available School Fund which is used for the cost of textbooks. The Foundation School Program is considered the main source of distributing funding and is a state-local funding program that aims to provide financial equality among schools. Local governments have long relied on the property tax as their main revenue source which meant this was how schools were primarily funded. The result of this was that localities with wealthy districts had well-financed schools whereas poorer localities with lower property values had less well-financed schools causing a disproportion in the education services provided to school children. This funding system came under fire in the state as seen in two court cases that led to reforms in education finance policy. The first case was *San Antonio v Rodriguez* (1973) which went to the US Supreme Court. In the case it was argued that the funding scheme used in Texas violated the Equal Protection Clause under the US Constitution because it did not distribute funds equally. The US Supreme Court determined that education is not a fundamental right under the US Constitution and that the unequal funding scheme did not discriminate against all the poor. Opponents of Texas's education finance policy then turned to the state constitution. In ***Edgewood v Kirby*** **(1989)**, a Texas court case, the funding scheme for education in Texas was again challenged but this time it was argued the funding scheme violated the Texas Constitution, Article VII Section 1 that requires the state to provide for free public schools. The Texas Supreme Court determined that the funding scheme based on property taxes was in violation of the state constitution. This led to a series of court cases and to actions taken by the Texas Legislature over the years. By 2006, after a number of special legislative sessions, a funding scheme was developed that would rely on a mix of property taxes, an increased business tax, $1.00 per pack tax on cigarettes and some monies from the general revenue fund. While this new funding scheme currently meets state constitutional standards, it is not perfect and the manner in which secondary and elementary education is funded will remain a divisive policy issue for years to come.

Higher education is dealt with by a different set of policies than elementary and secondary education. An early component of higher education policy can be seen with the establishment of the Permanent University Fund under the 1876 Texas Constitution that helps provide for two state university systems, the University of Texas and the Texas A&M University systems. The organization that oversees higher education policy in the state is the **Texas Higher Education Coordinating Board** (THECB) which was established by the Legislature in 1965. The THECB has a nine-member board appointed by the governor who serve six-year terms and a commissioner of higher education who is appointed by the board. The organization focuses on issues such as access and costs of higher education. In addition, universities have boards of regents or trustees that set guiding policies, in line with the rules and regulations established by the THECB, for their institutions. A current policy of the THECB is the 60x30TX plan which is focused on trying to get 60 percent of the 25–34-year-old population of Texas to have either a certificate or degree by the year 2030 and that the debt students graduate with should not be more than 60 percent of the wages they make during their first year of employment upon graduation.

Like with elementary and secondary education, the funding of higher education is an important policy concern. In 2003 the Texas Legislature deregulated higher education tuition which allows universities to alter tuition. The state had cut funding from higher education and the deregulation of tuition would allow universities to raise needed funds by raising tuition, required fees, and residence costs. This has led to problems for those who use higher education services, namely students, who must bear the additional cost burden of increased rates largely by borrowing in the form of student loans which may have a long-term impact on the economy of the state.

An important policy concern with higher education is with access, not only in regard to financial access, but to who has access to higher education services. Texas passed the Top 10% rule in 1997 requiring public colleges and universities to accept the top 10% of a graduating class. This was seen as a means of ensuring diversity by allowing the use of race as a factor in admissions. The Top 10% rule was altered for some universities such as UT-Austin to the top 8 percent in 2009 in order to allow for admittance of a broader range of students with skills and abilities that may not be apparent in regard to grades such as musical, artistic, and athletic abilities. The Top 10% rule came under fire in a series of court cases that went to the US Supreme Court but it was determined in the case *Fisher v University of Texas at Austin* (**2016**) that the program did not violate the Equal Protection Clause of the US Constitution. While the US Supreme Court upheld the policy, this does not mean the issue has been settled. There continues to be opposition by some in the state and several persons have called for a review of the policy including Governor Greg Abbott.

Social Welfare Policy

Social welfare policy involves the provision of social services to citizens by government. Those who receive social welfare benefits may include the elderly, disabled, unemployed, or may fall into the category of the working poor. According to the US Bureau of Labor Statistics, in 2013 10.5 million individuals in the United States could be categorized as working poor who "are people who spent at least 27 weeks in the labor force (that is, working or looking for work) but whose incomes still fell below the official poverty level."[5] Statistically in 2013, the working poor contain more part-time workers than full-time workers and are more likely to be women, African American or Hispanic, hold less than a high-school diploma, and have a child below the age of eighteen in the household. This is important to point out since it is essential to understand that social welfare policies are not geared simply toward those who do not work. Groups such as the working poor also benefit from such policies. The federal government provides a set of poverty guidelines that are often used to determine eligibility for social welfare programs such as the Supplemental Nutrition Assistance Program and the Children's Health Insurance Program, but not for cash assistance programs like Temporary Assistance to Needy Families. The federal poverty guideline for a family of four in 2016 was $24,300 and governments will often determine eligibility for social welfare programs by using 125 percent or 185 percent of the federal poverty guidelines as a baseline to determine whether a family is eligible for benefits.[6]

The main organization that addresses social welfare policy in Texas is the **Texas Health and Human Services Commission** (HHSC) which delivers a range of benefits to Texans including Medicaid and food benefits as well as providing services to those with disabilities, older Texans, and women. In September 2016, following Sunset legislation in 2015, the HHSC began a restructuring of its system in order to become more efficient and responsive to the public. HHSC has a number of divisions including the Department of Aging and Disability Services, Department of Assistive and

5.   U.S. Bureau of Labor Statistics, "A Profile of the Working Poor, 2013," BLS Reports, July, 2015, http://www.bls.gov/opub/reports/working-poor/archive/a-profile-of-the-working-poor-2013.pdf.

6.   U.S. Department of Health and Human Services, "Poverty Guidelines," last modified January 25, 2016, https://aspe.hhs.gov/poverty-guidelines.

Rehabilitative Services, Department of Family and Protective Services, and Department of State Health Services as well as the Internal Audit Division and an Office of Inspector General.

Policies briefly examined here are **Temporary Assistance to Needy Families** (TANF) and the **Supplemental Nutrition Assistance Program** (SNAP). TANF, which is administered by the HHSC, is a federal program administered by the states that provides cash payments to families in need. The state determines the eligibility standards, such as income, often based on the federal poverty guidelines. In Texas there is a requirement that participants agree to a Personal Responsibility Agreement that requires a child's guardian to agree to terms such as refraining from alcohol and drug abuse, if not employed to be training for or looking for employment, and to ensure children are vaccinated and attending school. TANF is specifically focused on families who have children eighteen or younger and factors such as income, assets, and child care/child support payments are used to determine eligibility. An example of the maximum amount that a family can receive in Texas under TANF is a single-parent home with one child may receive a maximum of $248 in monthly benefits to be used to help with a range of items including housing, utilities, and transportation.[7] SNAP is a social service program based on providing food benefits for those in need and cannot be used toward items such as alcohol or tobacco. While adults without children may be eligible for SNAP benefits, there are time frame limits under which they may receive benefits as well as work requirements. An example of the income requirements are that a family of two has a maximum monthly income limit of $2,203 in order to be eligible and the maximum monthly SNAP benefit amount is $357.[8] Social welfare programs such as TANF and SNAP are federal-state programs and allow Texas to set eligibility and benefit amounts that fall in line with the policy priorities of the state.

Environmental Policy

Environmental policy is implemented most frequently through the use of regulatory policy instruments. Environmental regulatory policy is often created through public agencies for the purpose of altering or controlling the behavior of industry. In 1993, Texas created the Texas Natural Resource Conservation Commission which was renamed the **Texas Commission on Environmental Quality** (TCEQ) in 2001.[9] The TCEQ is the state of Texas's environmental agency, similar to how the Environmental Protection Agency is for the federal government. TCEQ has three commissioners who serve six-year staggered terms, are appointed by the governor and have the role of establishing agency policy. The mission of the TCEQ is "to protect our state's public health and natural resources consistent with sustainable economic development. Our goal is clean air, clean water, and the safe management of waste."[10]

The federal Clean Air Act of 1970 helps create federal air quality standards and states are required to create and have state implementation plans (SIP) approved. Under amendments made to the Clean Air Act in 1990, if states do not comply and create a plan to meet the federal standards then they may be subject to penalties such as the loss of federal highway funding. The most recent revisions made to the Texas SIP occurred in 2007. In 2014, the EPA approved the **Texas Flexible**

---

7. Texas Health and Human Services Commission, "How to Get Help: TANF Cash Help," 2016, https://yourtexasbenefits.hhsc.texas.gov/programs/tanf/families.

8. Texas Health and Human Services Commission, "How to Get Help: SNAP Food Benefits," 2016, https://yourtexasbenefits.hhsc.texas.gov/programs/snap.

9. Texas Commission on Environmental Quality, "History of the TCEQ and Its Predecessor Agencies," last modified May 1, 2015, http://www.tceq.state.tx.us/about/tceqhistory.html.

10. Texas Commission on Environmental Quality, "Mission Statement and Agency Philosophy," last modified October 24, 2014, http://www.tceq.state.tx.us/about/mission.html.

Permit Program which involved clean air policy. The policy was rather contentious and the EPA and the TCEQ had been in a heated battle over the program. The approved program gives operators of plants flexibility in that they can create an overall cap on emissions of an individual emission limitation that will best serve the plant owners/operators.[11]

In addition to clean air, clean and available water is an important environmental policy area that the state addresses. Water is necessary for drinking, growing food, industrial use, and many more reasons. The Clean Water Act (Federal Water Pollution Control Act of 1972) is the federal law that imposes restrictions in order to clean up and maintain clean water. While the TCEQ handles enforcement of environmental regulations in regard to water, water policy itself is handled by numerous other groups. Water policy is complex and politically touchy especially between different parts of the state with some areas having access to larger quantities of water than others. Rights to water can depend on whether it is groundwater, generally belonging to the landowner, or surface water, considered to be owned by the state. The Texas Groundwater Act was passed in 1949 which created water conservation districts for the groundwater supply.[12] The Texas **1967 Water Rights Adjudication Act** created a water permit system for surface water that allows the TCEQ to issue such permits for rights to this water and the TCEQ must establish policy as to how to prioritize rights to water in times of need such as when a drought occurs.[13]

The TCEQ is involved in more than just clean air and clean water, for example environmental land issues such as wetlands protection, recycling, and waste disposal. Actions taken by the TCEQ in 2014 include adoption of "provisions to replace the state's dual inspection and registration sticker system with a single vehicle-registration sticker, and modifies the method used to collect the state's portion of vehicle emissions-inspection fees as required by HB 2305," modifying rules to allow prescribed burns to aid in prevention of wildfires and involvement in cleanup of Dallas Ebola-virus sites.[14]

Energy Policy

Energy is essential to many functions of everyday life such as keeping our buildings well-lighted, our cars on the road, and our electronic devices running smoothly. Energy production and consumption worldwide have been increasing. The United States consumes a good portion of this energy, most of it using fossil fuels rather than renewable resources. Energy crises continue to occur and the push to find additional and/or alternative sources for energy have been growing, and increasing attention has been given to the option of trying to reduce energy consumption. The biggest question today is how to resolve the energy crisis without wreaking havoc on the environment; essentially, what tradeoffs must take place in our policies to maintain our standard of living that account for both our energy needs and environmental quality. In order to maintain a balance between energy and environment, government will take action by instituting policies such as regulations, which are rules with the force of law meant to alter the actions and behaviors of others, taxation, which raises revenues

---

11. Texas Administrative Code, "Texas Administrative Code: Title 34 Public Finance, Part 1 Comptroller of Public Accounts, Chapter 19 State Energy Conservation Office," 2015, https://texreg.sos.state.tx.us/public/readtac$ext.View-TAC?tac_view=4&ti=34&pt=1&ch=19.
12. Texas Water Initiative, "Texas water law," Texas A&M University, 2014, http://texaswater.tamu.edu/water-law.
13. Texas Administrative Code, "Texas Administrative Code: Title 34 Public Finance. Part 1 Comptroller of Public Accounts, Chapter 19 State Energy Conservation Office," 2015, https://texreg.sos.state.tx.us/public/readtac$ext.View-TAC?tac_view=4&ti=34&pt=1&ch=19., Ibid.
14. Texas Commission on Environmental Quality, "History of the TCEQ and Its Predecessor Agencies," last modified May 1, 2015, http://www.tceq.state.tx.us/about/tceqhistory.html.

for public purposes but imposes costs on stakeholders, or subsidies, which can offset business costs and incentivize more production of a particular product as well as encourage further development. Which mechanism is used will depend on the goal of the policy. But in establishing policy, government will need to take into account **spillover effects**, meaning positive or negative externalities (i.e., effects from a transaction—buyer and seller—that impact people, in a good or a bad way, other than those directly involved in the transaction—third parties). Pollution is a good example of a negative externality, as it is the byproduct of industry that negatively impacts the broader community. The problem is that third parties, not those involved in the transaction, bear the cost. Taxes are one way of "internalizing the cost" for those involved in the transaction, but it is a double-edged sword. Pollution by the energy industry will still be an unintended consequence of the production of energy if regulation of the energy industry is too lax, while decreased energy production with no real environmental gain can result from excessive taxation.[15]

The amount of energy a state uses can be connected to its economic situation and its population. Often, a better economy and growing population signals an increased use of energy. In 2005 Texans spent about $114 billion on energy (about 11 percent of US energy expenditures), while 50.3 percent of energy in Texas was consumed by industry, 23.6 percent by transportation, 14 percent by residential, and 12.1 percent by commercial use.[16] Overall, Texas consumes more energy than any other single state in the United States, with California coming in second. Ensuring that there is enough energy to go around is essential to the functioning of the state. Traditional sources of energy include non-renewable fossil fuels such as oil, natural gas, and coal, while non-traditional sources of energy include renewables such as solar and wind power.[17]

We use oil a great deal in the US, taken both from within the country and that which we import from foreign sources. At a point in the foreseeable future, oil will run out. It is not renewable and thus will not magically re-appear. This raises many questions. Do we have a responsibility to reserve fuels for future generations? The oil and gas industry has been a major component of the Texas economy throughout much of the twentieth century. In addition to being a major industry in the state, several types of tax revenues are collected on oil and gas production, such as severance taxes and motor fuel taxes. Texas is the largest state producer of oil and gas in the United States.

The **Railroad Commission of Texas** (RRC) was first established in 1891 and, as noted earlier, is the oldest regulatory agency in Texas. The RRC "regulates the oil and gas industry, natural gas utilities, pipeline safety, the natural gas and hazardous liquid pipeline industry and surface coal and uranium mining in Texas" such as by issuing permits for oil and gas drilling.[18] The RRC contains three elected commissioners who serve six-year staggered terms. An example of how policy areas can overlap involves energy policy and border control policy where Chairman of the RRC David Porter implemented changes to policy that would allow RRC inspectors to carry weapons and satellite phones "to keep inspectors safe in pipeline areas in deep South Texas where armed smugglers may potentially come into contact with energy company employees, regulators and landowners."[19]

---

15. Peters, B. Guy, *American Public Policy: Promise and Performance* (Los Angeles: Sage, 2013).

16. Susan Combs, "The Energy Report," Texas Comptroller of Public Accounts, 2008, http://www.window.state.tx.us/specialrpt/energy/.

17. Anthony Champagne and Edward J. Harpham, *Governing Texas: An Introduction to Texas Politics* (New York: Norton & Co, 2013).

18. StateImpact, "What is the Railroad Commission of Texas?," *National Public Radio*, 2015, https://stateimpact.npr.org/texas/tag/railroad-commission-of-texas/.

19. Sergio Chapa, "Railroad Commission: Smugglers using pipeline routes as trafficking corridors," *San Antonio Business Journal*, last modified June 26, 2015, http://www.bizjournals.com/sanantonio/news/2015/06/26/railroad-commission-smugglersusing-pipeline.html.

In the United States, Texas is the largest producer and consumer of natural gas. Of the fossil fuels that we use, natural gas burns cleaner than both oil and coal, but it continues to contribute to environmental problems such as air pollution. It is not just the use of these fossil fuels, or that they will one day run out, that is environmentally problematic. The manner in which we gather these fuels can also create major problems. Numerous issues overlap energy and environmental policy, especially in regard to the potential environmental problems caused by gathering certain forms of energy. A current controversy in the state of Texas has to do with environmental concerns surrounding a method of extraction of natural gas called fracking. The process involves a mixture of chemicals, sand, and pressurized water being drilled into rock to unlock the gas. The energy industry argues that the practice is safe while opponents believe that not only does it create aesthetic problems but that it overuses water and leads to water pollution. In May 2015, Governor Greg Abbott signed House Bill 40 that prohibits cities from placing bans on fracking. The governor argued it will allow for more consistency in energy policy.[20] This issue was placed on the state policy agenda in reaction to a public movement against fracking having achieved a policy victory in the town of Denton, where fracking was first used in Texas. In November 2014, the town banned fracking within its limits by a 58 percent town vote. This particular policy has pitted state against local government and shows the complexity of energy and environmental policy in Texas.[21]

Another fossil fuel used in the United States is coal. Coal is bountiful in the US, and the US is one of the largest producers of coal-fired energy in the world. However, it is also the dirtiest of all fossil fuels and environmentally the most damaging. Each president since Nixon has called for an increased use of coal due to its abundance in the US, and this applies to the current administration as well. Texas has large amounts of lower-grade coal; however, most Texas plants burn higher-grade coal brought in from out of state.[22]

Nuclear power accounts for a significant percentage of the power generated in the United States, and many people began to turn back to it recently. Nuclear power does not create the same emission problems as fossil fuels, but environmental hazards occur in its production, and it produces a great deal of radioactive waste that has to be properly disposed of in long-term storage facilities. Many state and localities which could house the storage facilities oppose locating them there. This results in the **NIMBY effect** (Not In My Back Yard), a policy implementation problem where most people want a particular policy or service, but they do not want the facilities that provide the service located near where they live. We see this problem crop up when cities have to locate major highways, landfills, and industrial parks. Another major concern with nuclear energy is the cost of building facilities to ensure safe production. Safety technology and protocols have improved since the Three Mile Island partial nuclear reactor meltdown in 1979, the only such incident in US history. However, the disaster at the Fukushima Daiichi nuclear plant in Japan on March 11, 2011, following an earthquake and tsunami, has stymied somewhat the promotion of nuclear power as a safe alternative to fossil fuels, much like the Deepwater Horizon disaster tampered interest in drilling offshore immediately after the disaster.[23] There are several nuclear power facilities in Texas and uranium is mined in South Texas and used to fuel plants.

---

20. Reuters, "Texas Governor Prohibits Cities and Towns from Banning Fracking," *The Huffington Post Politics*, May 18, 2015, http://www.huffingtonpost.com/2015/05/18/texas-frackingban_n_7310072.html.

21. Marice Richter, "Denton, Texas Voters are First in State to Ban Fracking," *The Huffington Post Politics*, November 5, 2014, http://www.huffingtonpost.com/2014/11/05/denton-texas-fracking-ban_n_6106484.html.

22. Dwight F. Henderson, and Diana J. Kleiner, "Coal and Lignite Mining," Texas State Historical Association, 2010, https://tshaonline.org/handbook/online/articles/dkc03.

23. WNA, "Safety of Nuclear Power Reactors," *Agenta Rising*, last modified May, 2016 http://www.world-nuclear.org/information-library/safety-and-security/safety-of-plants/safety-of-nuclear-power-reactors.aspx

The Texas agency focused on broader energy policy is the **State Energy Conservation Office** (SECO) whose mission "is to maximize energy efficiency while protecting the environment. SECO administers and delivers a variety of energy efficiency and renewable energy programs that significantly reduce energy cost and consumption in the institutional, industrial, transportation and residential sectors."[24] SECO, established in 2002, is under the control and direction of the Texas Comptroller of Public Accounts. SECO has a variety of programs including a revolving loan program which provides a specialized form of financing for energy and water efficiency improvements in public facilities, a pollution mitigation program, an alternative fuels program for public and private fleets, and the Pantex program which protects the health and safety of citizens connected with the Pantex Plant which assembles and disassembles nuclear weapons in Carson County.[25]

At this point, no single renewable energy source can provide all the energy required in the US. However, a combination of energy sources may be the key to sustaining energy production. Solar power is basically thermal power harnessed from the sun. Solar power has gone through phases of popularity in the US (meaning when gas is cheaper, it is less popular). Solar power can produce a great deal of energy in an efficient manner; however, it requires a certain climate (sunny), space, and may lead to heat island externalities that can potentially damage local ecosystems that may already be under stress. Another alternative source that has grown dramatically in recent years, especially in Texas, is wind energy. Wind is by no means a new energy source, but the growth and use of wind farms in the US is fairly new. While wind does not produce the emissions problems of other energy sources, it can be costly, can upset patterns of migratory birds, and the aesthetics of wind farms can produce NIMBY effects. In addition, biomass can create fuels such as ethanol, biodiesel, and electricity. As of 2008, Texas was leading the nation in installed wind power, as a producer of biodiesel, and is one of the largest producers of solar power.[26]

Conclusion

This chapter addressed a number of different substantive policy areas that the state of Texas is actively involved in. Fiscal policy is a primary tool of government and the state has engaged in a range of revenue and spending policies that have kept state taxes relatively low. Education policy at the elementary and secondary and higher education levels is of concern to citizens throughout the state and often focuses on how policies are funded and who has access to those services. Another area of policy Texas is involved in is providing social services to citizens through social welfare policies. Finally, this chapter looked at the areas of environmental policy and energy policy, two policy areas that often overlap. Texas must continue to consider how these two policy areas must be balanced in order to maintain the health and prosperity of its citizens, a goal of many public policies that state is engaged in.

---

24. Glenn, Hegar, "State Energy Conservation Office: About this Site," Texas Comptroller of Public Accounts, 2015, http://seco.cpa.state.tx.us/about/.
25. Ibid.
26. Susan Combs, "The Energy Report," Texas Comptroller of Public Accounts, 2008, http://www.window.state.tx.us/specialrpt/energy/.

Key Terms

Fiscal policy
Regressive tax
Progressive tax
Economic Stabilization Fund
Comptroller of Public Accounts
Legislative Budget Board
Texas Education Agency
Edgewood v Kirby (1989)
Texas Higher Education Coordinating Board
Fisher v University of Texas at Austin (2016)
Texas Health and Human Services Commission
Temporary Assistance to Needy Families
Supplemental Nutrition Assistance Program
Texas Commission on Environmental Quality
Texas Flexible Permit Program
1967 Water Rights Adjudication Act
Spillover effects
Railroad Commission of Texas
NIMBY effect
State Energy Conservation Office

References

Acosta, Palomo Teresa. "Edgewood ISD v. Kirby." *Handbook of Texas Online.* Last modified March 25, 2016. http://www.tshaonline.org/handbook/online/articles/jre02.

Champagne, Anthony, and Edward J. Harpham. 2013. *Governing Texas: An Introduction to Texas Politics.* New York: Norton & Co.

Chapa, Sergio. "Railroad Commission: Smugglers using pipeline routes as trafficking corridors." *San Antonio Business Journal.* Last modified June 26, 2015. http://www.bizjournals.com/sanantonio/news/2015/06/26/railroad-commission-smugglersusing-pipeline.html.

Combs, Susan. 2008. "The Energy Report." Texas Comptroller of Public Accounts. http://www.window.state.tx.us/specialrpt/energy/.

Costello, TJ, David Green, and Patrick Graves. "The Texas Economic Stabilization Fund: Saving for Rainy Days." Last modified September, 2016. https://www.comptroller.texas.gov/economy/fiscal-notes/2016/september/rainy-day.php.

Hegar, Glenn. 2015. "State Energy Conservation Office: About this Site." Texas Comptroller of Public Accounts. http://seco.cpa.state.tx.us/about/.

Henderson, Dwight F. and Diana J. Kleiner. 2010. "Coal and Lignite Mining." Texas State Historical Association. https://tshaonline.org/handbook/online/articles/dkc03.

Kaiser Family Foundation. 2016. "State Health Facts: Total State Expenditures (in millions)." http://kff.org/other/state-indicator/total-state-spending/?currentTimeframe=0&sortModel=%7B%22colId%22:%-22Total%20State%20Expenditures%20(in%20millions)%22,%22sort%22:%22desc%22%7D.

Legislative Budget Board. "Summary of Appropriations for the 2016-2017 Biennium." February, 2016. http://www.lbb.state.tx.us/Documents/Budget/Session_Code_84/2580_84_BillSummary.pdf.

—. "Fiscal Size-Up 2016-2017 Biennium." May, 2016. http://www.lbb.state.tx.us/Documents/Publications/Fiscal_SizeUp/Fiscal_SizeUp.pdf.

Peters, B. Guy. 2013. *American Public Policy: Promise and Performance*. Los Angeles: Sage.

Reuters. "Texas Governor Prohibits Cities and Towns from Banning Fracking." *The Huffington Post Politics*. May 18, 2015. http://www.huffingtonpost.com/2015/05/18/texas-frackingban_n_7310072.html.

Richter, Marice. "Denton, Texas Voters are First in State to Ban Fracking." *The Huffington Post Politics*. November 5, 2014. http://www.huffingtonpost.com/2014/11/05/denton-texas-fracking-ban_n_6106484.html.

StateImpact. 2015. "What is the Railroad Commission of Texas?" *National Public Radio*. https://stateimpact.npr.org/texas/tag/railroad-commission-of-texas/.

Texas Administrative Code. 2015. "Texas Administrative Code: Title 34 Public Finance. Part 1 Comptroller of Public Accounts. Chapter 19 State Energy Conservation Office." https://texreg.sos.state.tx.us/public/readtac$ext.ViewTAC?tac_view=4&ti=34&pt=1&ch=19.

Texas Commission on Environmental Quality. "History of the TCEQ and Its Predecessor Agencies." Last modified May 1, 2015. http://www.tceq.state.tx.us/about/tceqhistory.html.

—. "Mission Statement and Agency Philosophy." Last modified October 24, 2014. http://www.tceq.state.tx.us/about/mission.html.

Texas Comptroller of Public Accounts. "Economic Stabilization Fund." June, 2016. https://www.comptroller.texas.gov/transparency/budget/docs/EconomicStabilizationFund.pdf.

Texas Education Agency. 2016. "About TEA: Welcome and Overview." http://tea.texas.gov/About_TEA/Welcome_and_Overview/.

—. 2016. "Student Testing and Accountability: STAAR Resources." http://tea.texas.gov/student.assessment/staar/.

Texas Health and Human Services. 2016. "About HHS." https://hhs.texas.gov/about-hhs.

—. 2016. "How to Get Help: TANF Cash Help." https://yourtexasbenefits.hhsc.texas.gov/programs/tanf/families.

—. 2016. "How to Get Help: SNAP Food Benefits." https://yourtexasbenefits.hhsc.texas.gov/programs/snap.

Texas Higher Education Coordinating Board. 2016. "Texas Higher Education Coordinating Board." http://www.thecb.state.tx.us/.

Texas Municipal League. 2016. "Local sales tax bill gives cities increased financial flexibility." http://www.tml.org/legis_updates/local-sales-tax-bill-gives-cities-increased-financial-flexibility.

Texas Water Initiative. 2014. "Texas water law." Texas A&M University. http://texaswater.tamu.edu/water-law.

U.S. Bureau of Labor Statistics. "A Profile of the Working Poor, 2013." BLS Reports. July, 2015. http://www.bls.gov/opub/reports/working-poor/archive/a-profile-of-the-working-poor-2013.pdf.

U.S. Department of Health and Human Services. "Poverty Guidelines." Last modified January 25, 2016. https://aspe.hhs.gov/poverty-guidelines.

Watkins, Matthew and Neena Satija. "Fisher ruling could spur changes to Texas' Top 10 Percent Rule." *Texas Tribune Online*. June 23, 2016. https://www.texastribune.org/2016/06/23/could-scotus-ruling-help-end-top-10-percent-rule/.

WNA. "Safety of Nuclear Power Reactors," *Agenta Rising*. Last modified May, 2016, http://www.world-nuclear.org/info/Safety-and-Security/Safety-of-Plants/Safety-ofNuclear-Power-Reactors/.

Exercise 6.1 ■ Multiple Choice

1. Which of the following is true in regard to fiscal policy in Texas?
   a. Texas is not required to balance the state budget.
   b. Texas does not have a state income tax.
   c. The state relies on a statewide property tax as its main source of revenue.
   d. Fiscal policy in Texas relies on a progressive tax system.

2. Which of the following provided a way for local governments to reformulate the manner in which they determined the amount of additional city sales tax that they could add to the general state sales tax, thus giving local governments more flexibility in their fiscal policies?
   a. Texas Constitution
   b. 1967 Local Sales and Use Tax
   c. House Bill 40 (2015)
   d. House Bill 157 (2015)

3. Who of the following is responsible for determining and certifying the expected revenues for the next budget cycle in Texas?
   a. Comptroller of Public Accounts
   b. Texas Legislature
   c. Legislative Budget Board
   d. State of Texas Auditor

4. Which of the following organizations oversees issues such as distribution of funding to schools and the assessment and testing of students under programs such as STAAR?
   a. State Board of Education
   b. Texas Higher Education Coordinating Board
   c. State Board of Regents
   d. Texas Education Agency

5. In this court case it was determined that the reliance on property taxes to fund elementary and secondary education in the state of Texas was a violation of the Texas Constitution which provides for free public schools.
   a. *San Antonio v Rodriguez* (1973)
   b. *Edgewood v Kirby* (1989)
   c. *Hopwood v Texas* (1996)
   d. *Fisher v University of Texas at Austin* (2016)

6. In this court case it was determined that the Top 10% Rule used in Texas to promote diversity in higher education was not a violation of the Equal Protection Clause of the US Constitution.
   a. *San Antonio v Rodriguez* (1973)
   b. *Edgewood v Kirby* (1989)
   c. *Hopwood v Texas* (1996)
   d. *Fisher v University of Texas at Austin* (2016)

7. Which of the following social welfare programs that is administered by the states provides cash payments to needy families for items such as housing and transportation?
   a. Medicaid
   b. Temporary Assistance to Needy Families
   c. Unemployment insurance
   d. Supplemental Nutrition Assistance Program

8. Which of the following is true?
   a. Supplemental Nutrition Assistance Program benefits cannot be used toward the purchase of alcohol or tobacco.
   b. Texas does not require recipients of Temporary Assistance to Needy Families benefits to agree to a Personal Responsibility Agreement.
   c. Only the unemployed receive social welfare benefits.
   d. All of the above.

9. Which Texas agency is tasked with the responsibility of ensuring that air quality meets required standards?
   a. Texas Commission on Air Quality
   b. Texas Commission on Environmental Quality
   c. Texas Clean Air Agency
   d. Texas Environmental Protection Agency

10. Under House Bill 40, Governor Abbott gave which governmental entity power over fracking policy?
    a. Municipalities
    b. Independent districts
    c. Townships
    d. State government

Exercise 6.2　■　Research Exercise

It is often useful to compare where states rank in terms of their policy programs. For this exercise you will choose four categories of policy issues to compare Texas with using information provided by the Texas Comptroller of Public Accounts.

Go to the website: http://www.comptroller.texas.gov/economy/50state/

The website provides a comparison of the fifty states using a scorecard approach on issues such as business and the workforce, quality of life, population and demographics, economic indicators, and tax debt. Choose four of the categories and one item under each category. For example, you could choose "Business and Workforce" and underneath that choose "Best and Worst States for Business." For each one explain where Texas ranks in the spectrum and the ranking and key takeaways of the ranking as discussed on the website. Do you believe Texas needs to improve its ranking in the category, or if Texas is the top ranked state, do you believe Texas needs to make any policy changes in order to maintain that status? Explain your response.

Exercise 6.3 ■ Writing Exercise

If you were responsible for developing an energy policy for Texas, what would the policy look like? How much would you rely on traditional non-renewable resources? How much on non-traditional, renewable resources? Be sure to be realistic and consider the pros and cons of all sources, meaning who would be for and against your plan and would it be likely to get passed. Your response should be a minimum of one page and be sure to include an introduction, conclusion, and a list of any sources that you use.

coalition of more than fifty organizations working to prevent obesity, filed an open letter in opposition to the changes. Miller responded that it "isn't about french fries, it's about freedom."

The Texas Public Schools Nutrition Policy, and its promulgation, implementation, evaluation, and political reassessment, is an excellent example of the dynamics at play in modern state public policy. From the actors, institutions, and agencies involved at the federal, state, and local levels, we can see the impact of fiscal federalism in directing and strongly influencing policy as implemented at the local levels. The federal government does not merely dictate policy in areas where federal constitutional supremacy preempts state policy. Even in areas traditionally within the sphere of state action, such as the policy powers, the federal government has substantial influence. The Texas Agricultural Department has to conform to federal guidelines when setting the Texas public school nutrition policy, because it is largely funded by the federal government through programs like Smart Snacks and the National School Lunch Program. That said, the processes and dynamics of modern state public policy still allow for independent state action, even in policy areas with significant federal involvement. The TPSNP demonstrates that state agencies have discretion to follow and implement state and local priorities distinct from the federal government, such as the rule on deep-fat fryers. This example further highlights the role of policy science in studying implemented public policies and helping agencies evaluate the effect and effectiveness of policies put in place. It shows us the role that actors outside of the official policymaking process, such as interest groups like the Partnership for a Healthy Texas, can have in shaping Texas public policy. And finally, it teaches us the importance of politics and political pressure in assessing policies and initiating changes in policy direction and policy priorities. We will return to this example throughout the chapter to help elucidate the theories of public policy.

Theories of the Policy Process: From the Policy Stages Heuristic to the Advocacy Coalition Framework

There are many theories of public policy that attempt to define and describe its actors, processes, and outputs. The shared commonality between these theories is a focus on what government's do—the policies and policymaking of government agencies. Harold Lasswell promulgated the first theories of policy science, arguing that the study of public policy should focus on problem-solving and practical politics. The iconic theoretical description of the policy process, developed from Lasswell's writings, is the **policy stages heuristic**. The PSH envisions the policy process as a series of linear, sequential steps or stages where a public policy is developed, instituted, implemented, and evaluated.:

Policy Stages Heuristic

1. Policy Agenda Setting and Problem Definition
2. Policy Formulation
3. Policy Adoption
4. Policy Implementation
5. Policy Evaluation

The PSH is a simple, understandable, and useful way of depicting discrete aspects of the policy-making process. Agenda Setting covers the problem identification and definition process where policymakers perceive a political problem, define policy goals in reacting to the problem, examine and identify potential policies to address that problem, and decide which issues deserve more attention than others. We saw policymaking in action in this stage with the studies and political leaders who identified the problem of increasing childhood obesity in Texas. Policy Formulation encompasses the aspect of policymaking where policymakers set objectives, identify costs and benefits with implementing certain rules and policies over others, and select appropriate policy instruments to deliver on the policy goals. This is the stage where the Texas Department of Agriculture was in action, developing the Texas Public Schools Nutrition Policy and determining that it would have rules such as the deep-fryer ban and the restrictions on competitive food delivery in public schools. Policy Adoption is the stage of the policy process whereby the proposed policy is made official and publicized through official channels. In this stage, Texas publicized the policy on official state media, such as the TDA website, distributed the policies to public schools in Texas, and published reports describing and analyzing the new policy and its requirements. The Policy Implementation stage of policymaking is where the street-level actors, such as public schools in Texas in the TPSNP example, take responsibility for complying with the new policy, providing resources such that these actors can comply with the policy, and ensuring that policy decisions are carried out according to the directives. Finally, Policy Evaluation involves assessing the extent to which the policy has been successful and effective in ameliorating the problem as identified, assessing how well and completely the policy has been implemented, and considering whether the policy should be continued, modified, or discontinued. Feedback from stakeholders and citizens, academic and agency studies of implementation effectiveness, and studies of policy effectiveness are the bread and butter of policy evaluation. Policy evaluation can be external or internal to the agency that implemented the policy. We saw internal policy evaluation in the audits conducted by TDA of public schools to determine the extent of implementation of TPSNP, and we saw external policy evaluation with the academic studies assessing how effective the TPSNP had been in making school food healthier, and in the published data on the childhood obesity trend after the program was instituted. The changes made to the TPSNP in reaction to implementation of the policy are also part and parcel of policy evaluation, as policymakers decided to discontinue certain parts of the policy. Generally the policy stages are conceived as a recursive **policy cycle**, where policy evaluation leads once again to agenda setting and problem definition.

Critics of the PSH argue that the policymaking process is neither discrete nor sequential. They point to its top-down, legalistic approach as a defect in that it neglects to account for the interconnected nature of lawmaking and policy formulation. And they argue that the policy stages occur nonlinearly, that agenda setting, policy formulation, policy adoption, policy implementation, and policy evaluation often occur simultaneously. For example, note that the TPSNP was being implemented at the same time it was being evaluated in academic studies and the policy problem was being reformulated on the political agenda. Lastly, critics point out that the PSH approach tends to de-emphasize the importance of political values in influencing the policymaking process at each stage. Policies are often evaluated on terms having little to do with their effectiveness in addressing the policy problem they were developed to fix. For example, consider the fact that parts of the TPSNP were discontinued, not because of policy evaluation by the agencies charged with its implementation that showed it had been ineffective, but rather because of political considerations and interests that activated to reconceptualize the policy "problem" in terms of permitting discretion for schools in setting their own policies (i.e., freedom, rather than in terms of the effectiveness of TPSNP in combating obesity). These critics certainly have made a number of good points arguing against a strict adherence to the PSH depiction of the policymaking process, but it remains a useful tool for understanding and describing important aspects of the policymaking process.

Policy science researchers have developed a number of alternative theories to better describe and explain the policy process. Institutional rational choice (IRC) is a family of policymaking theories that focus on institutional rules and how they shape the behavior of policy actors, who are presumed to be goal-seeking and self-interested. We see these theories frequently used to help us understand the relationship between legislatures, which make the laws, and agencies, which implement the laws through policies and rules. IRC helps us understand, for example, why the TPSNP was modified in ways that may make it less effective as a tool to fight obesity by lawmakers and political leaders such as Representative King and Commissioner Miller. Variously referred to as incrementalism, the **Garbage Can Model**, and the Multiple-Streams Framework (MSF), this class of policy theories views the policy process as composed of three streams of actors and processes: a problem stream (data and analysis of policy problems and their definitions), a policy stream (proponents of solutions), and a politics stream (elections and elected officials). These theories have the advantage of explicitly incorporating politics as a factor in the policymaking process and in not imposing a sequential or discrete model of policymaking. Incremental theories envision a mostly undirected policy process which is characterized by small, often random, changes to the status quo policy. Generally the streams operate independently, except when a **policy window** opens where **policy entrepreneurs** can operate across streams and thus make more substantial changes than normal. A variation on incremental theory is the Punctuated-Equilibrium Framework (PEF), which depicts the policymaking process as one characterized by long periods of incremental change punctuated by a relatively brief period of major change. Hence, policy change proceeds in a step-like manner; though the status quo can move up or down on the relative policy dimensions. MSF and PEF are not incompatible theories. Indeed, policy windows opening to permit major change, as described by MSF, is quite similar to the punctuated-equilibrium concept of the PEF.

There are other important alternative models of the policymaking process. **Policy network** and **policy diffusion** theories focus on the interconnected actors and institutions that contribute to a public policy along the federal-state vertical and state-to-state horizontal policy dimensions as a way of mapping policy adoption across multiple institutions and policy learning over time. This theory would have a great deal of utility in understanding why Texas was out in front of the federal government and other states on public school nutrition, and why it adopted a stricter set of nutrition guidelines than those adopted by other institutions implementing public school nutrition regulations. The last policy theory we will cover is the Advocacy Coalition Framework, which focuses on the interaction of advocacy coalitions, actors from a variety of institutions who share a set of policy beliefs, acting within a policy subsystem where change can come from within (i.e., the adoption of stricter nutrition standards by TDA) or from without (the elimination of the deep-fat fryer provision by the Texas Legislature). The above constitute most of the major theories of the policymaking process. They each provide important insights into how the policymaking process occurs and give us useful theoretical frameworks to shape our understanding of how Texas state and local policy changes and evolves.

Policy Institutions, Actors, and Instruments in Texas

While having a theory of the policymaking process and why change in policies occur is an important step in understanding public policy, it is equally important to identify who are the major actors in the policy process, what institutions are responsible for formulating and implementing policy in Texas, and what instruments they use to give Texas public policies effect. Most public policy theories treat individual, group, and institutional actors as the key causal and explanatory factors in understanding why certain policy problems are focused upon, why certain policies are chosen, and how the implementation and evaluation processes take shape. We will discuss five important public policy actors: (1) citizens and citizen activists, (2) interest groups, (3) stakeholders, (4) public agencies, and (5) elected local and state government officials.

Stated simply, an actor in public policy ranges from an individual concerned citizen taking some kind of action (attending a public hearing, distributing flyers, calling or writing their elected official, blogging about it on the Internet, etc.) to a massive federal bureaucracy, like the US Department of Agriculture. Citizen activists acting as individuals or in concert with others, usually have small effects on public policy at the local level, however they can sometimes have a substantial effect when sufficient attention is given to them. Recently, citizen activists such as Michael Bishop, owner of an East Texas farm, have spoken out against the international oil delivery project known as the Keystone XL pipeline. Exercising the power of eminent domain, the power of the state to condemn a citizen's property for public purposes in exchange for just compensation, part of Bishop's twenty acres near Nacogdoches were seized in order to facilitate construction of the pipeline. Demonstrators have attempted to call attention to what they say is the negative environmental impact of the pipeline in East Texas by organizing protests at the construction site, organized letter writing campaigns, and a march in Washington, D.C. To this date, the Keystone XL pipeline project remains politically controversial. It did not receive approval during the Obama administration, but in 2017, President Donald Trump approved the project through an executive order.

Interest groups are a set-up in organization and impact on the policy process from citizen activists. Interest groups play a critical role in organizing public opinion and putting pressure on public officials on policy in most democratic systems. In Texas, interest groups play a critical and influential role in the policy process. Thomas and Hrebenar rated states on the strength of interest groups in the Union ranging from "dominant" to "subordinate" on a five-point scale. Texas rated a four out of five (dominant/complementary) along with sixteen other states in terms of interest group power in state politics. Only nine states were rated higher (dominant) in interest group strength on the scale than Texas was ranked. Interest groups such as Raise Your Hand Texas, founded by San Antonio grocery mogul Charles Butt, have been influential on state educational policy and pushing for private school vouchers. Groups such as Public Citizen Texas have pushed hard against energy projects like the Keystone XL pipeline, while business interest groups like the Texas Association of Business and the Texas National Federation of Independent Business argue for them. Interest groups often advocate on behalf of **policy stakeholders** (persons, groups, or organizations that stand to gain or lose based on the outcome of the implementation of a public policy). For example, Mr. Bishop, the owner of the property condemned in order to build the XL pipeline, and TransCanda Co., the multinational corporation building the pipeline, both are stakeholders in the policymaking related to the project's approval.

Public agencies are the lynchpin of bureaucratic politics and are the key actor in the policymaking process. While not a constitutionally instituted branch of government, public agencies are permanent public organizations, usually located in the executive branch of government, given the responsibility of oversight of a policy area, administration of public policy, and the promulgation of rules and regulations in a policy area. Agencies are a unique form of governmental institution, as they serve legislative (rulemaking), executive (enforcement, audits), and judicial functions (imposition of fines, injunctions) in the policy process. There are 171 state bureaucratic agencies, courts, commissions, and boards currently listed by TRAIL, the Texas Records, Archives and Information Locator service. The Department of Criminal Justice is the largest state government employer. Other major Texas state agencies include the aforementioned Texas Department of Agriculture, the Department of Education, the Department of Rural Affairs, the Department of Banking, the Department of Human Services, the Department of Transportation, and the Department of Public Safety. In addition to departments, the Texas Constitution commits regulatory responsibility to a number of important boards and commissions. Texas state **boards and commissions** are either elected or appointed by the governor, and they have a significant influence on Texas public policy and, in some cases, national policy. For example, given the size and importance of the Texas school system, the Texas State Board of Education, in setting policy for public school textbooks in Texas, has a strong impact on the composition of public school textbooks at the national level. This means its decisions are often politically controversial. The Texas Railroad Commission is an historically significant commission, as it was one of the first Texas state commissions, and it plays an important part in Texas energy policy today in making decisions on Texas natural resources and economic development. Ironically, the Texas Railroad Commission no longer has responsibility for railroads, that policy responsibility having been transferred to the Texas Department of Transportation.

Last but not least, elected government officials are key policy actors in the policymaking process. Responsible for making and enforcing the laws at the state and local levels, government officials are the prime movers in policy agenda setting and have significant influence over the formulation and implementation stages through their oversight (legislature) and appointments to office (executive) of public agencies. And government officials have a significant role in the evaluation process as well, as we saw Rep. King in the "deep fryer" controversy with respect to the Texas Public Schools Nutrition Policy.

Just as important as identifying the important actors in the policymaking process is understanding the methods and tools that policymakers have at hand to affect public policy. Policy instruments or policy tools are means or devices governments use to put policies into effect. Consider the childhood obesity problem mentioned earlier in the chapter. What tools did the TDA use to implement its policy? It provided monies to public schools to implement a school lunch program, partly funded by the federal government. It used audits to determine the extent of public implementation of the policy. It used expert studies to support the policy. And then it used fines to punish schools for violating those policies. Each of those is a policy instrument used by TDA to give effect to the nutrition policy. There are other policy instruments that could have been brought to bear on the problem of childhood obesity. For example, an advertising campaign to raise awareness for childhood obesity could have been deployed, or a tax on fatty foods could have been imposed. There is a multiplicity of policy instruments that policymakers can use to give their policies affect.

There are four primary classifications of policy instruments we will discuss here: (1) direct benefits, (2) regulation and monitoring, (3) expertise and advice, and (4) advertising. As we saw with the national school lunch program, direct benefits, through grants, subsidies, or other material benefits are an important component of fiscal federalism and of policymaking in general. Through rules and regulations and monitoring compliance with those rules (e.g., TPSNP), agencies can inform stakeholders and policy-relevant institutions of the steps they must take to comply with policy, assess the degree of compliance, and take appropriate steps when actors are out of line with expectations. This type of policy instrument was illustrated when the TDA imposed fines on public schools who failed the TPSNP audit. Expertise and advice is an important and often undervalued policy instrument in the toolbox of public agencies, as their narrow focus on a policy area allows them to generate a great deal of expertise and practical knowledge in a particular policy area. Public agencies also can commission academic studies, such as the studies on the implementation of TPSNP mentioned earlier in the chapter, to determine the effectiveness of the implemented policies, evaluate those studies, and support the efficacy of their policymaking to political officeholders. Similarly, advertising, through public campaigns, public service announcements, and other instruments designed to disseminate information to the public, is an effective way of promoting the voluntary adoption of preferred policies by the public at large and making them more aware of identified policy problems.

Policy Implementation and Evaluation in Texas

Policy Decision-Making

After a policy issue is placed on the agenda, a decision must be made about how to address the problem. These decisions can be quite complex and require specialized knowledge, as well as entail costs and require trade-offs. We traditionally think of rational decision-making much like the policy process itself, where decision-making is a step-by-step process that begins by defining the problem. Unfortunately, in making decisions on public policy, decision-makers may not have all of the information necessary to make the right decision consistent with their goals (i.e., we do not know the exact causes of poverty), may have little time to make the decision and gather additional information (for example, in deciding where to prioritize resources being sent to disaster areas), and may lack the necessary cognitive skills or specialized knowledge to make a decision (for example, in deciding which space exploration concept to fund—decision-makers are not all rocket scientists). In these situations, where decision-making is limited by time, knowledge, and skills, decision-makers must operate under **bounded rationality**, a phrase coined by Nobel laureate Herbert Simon, where decision-makers satisfice (rather than satisfy) elements of the decision-making process. In other words, they try to choose the best option they can come up with, given their limited knowledge, abilities, and circumstances.

The procedures used to make policy decisions and the actual decisions made must be considered legitimate actions of government, meaning the public believes the decisions made and actions taken are within the proper powers of the government body making the decisions. When this legitimacy is not present in government decisions, the public may lose confidence in government and the authority of government to make policy decisions can be reduced.

Traditionally we think of legislatures making policy decisions through law and then those who work in government agencies, a.k.a. bureaucrats, as the ones who implement the laws. However, decisions on policy are made at many levels. For example, Congress passed the federal Clean Air Act requiring the implementation of national ambient air quality standards, but the Environmental Protection Agency (EPA) makes the specific decisions as to how many parts per billion of a particular pollutant can be in the air through the creation of administrative rules, policies that explain how laws are implemented.

Policy Implementation

One of the first things to consider with the implementation of policy is that it requires some type of organization to put the policy into place. This is where many of your institutions come into play. When designing the policy to implement, decision-makers need to ensure that an agency exists to put that policy into place. Sometimes a single agency will exist to address a policy problem, but at other times there will be multiple agencies often at different levels of government that have responsibility for implementing a particular policy. For example, while the EPA makes decisions on NAAQS, it is the Texas Commission on Environmental Quality that creates a plan for air quality at the state level, referred to as a state implementation plan (SIP), that must be approved by the federal EPA. Later in the chapter we will see how problematic intergovernmental relations can lead to difficulties in implementing policy when we look more closely at the EPA, TCEQ, and clean air policy, and in particular the difficulty of state versus federal implementation of immigration policy. The organizations that implement public policy are thus often fragmented in the sense of multiple organizations having responsibilities but no single or centralized agency is in control, making accountability difficult. In addition to vertical institutional problems, there can also be horizontal institutional problems, where agencies at the same level of government must coordinate together to institute a policy. For example, we see this when the TCEQ and the Texas Department of Agriculture work together on water policy issues during times of drought.

Ideally, an organization that is implementing a policy will be structured in a way where all elements of the organization are following the same rules, are willing to take action, and have all necessary time, knowledge, and communication skills. However, this is rarely the case. Issues that impact the implementation of public policy include how specific the legislation is that established the policy (specificity in legislation is a double-edged sword: a law with a lot of specifics can be difficult to pass, but more general, broadly defined laws allow for a lot of interpretation and administrative discretion in implementing the law), the accuracy of knowledge about the causes for the policy problem, adequate information about the chosen policy (such as whether a new technology will function appropriately), and lack of funding.

Policy Evaluation

Evaluation of public policies is the process of determining the results or consequences of a particular policy. With policy evaluation, you are attempting to ensure that the goals of a policy have been met in the most efficient and effective manner possible, and if not, what changes can or should be made to that policy. One of the main problems with evaluating public policies is that it can be unclear what the specific goal is and how to go about measuring that goal. For example, what are the goals of a drug control policy; is it the number of persons arrested and incarcerated, a reduction in recidivism rate, or a change in the rate of persons entering drug rehabilitation facilities (and with that, would you want more or fewer persons in the facility to show the success of a drug control policy)? Another concern with goals is whether a goal could be achieved at all. For example, is it practical to set a goal of zero unemployment? There are frequently people who choose not to enter the workforce (i.e., people who choose to stay home with family, students who choose to take a semester off and not work, or those who are in the process of looking for a new job). Would a zero unemployment rate be a realistic policy goal?

If we are able to clearly determine what the goals of a policy are, how to measure the success of goal-achievement, and whether the policy implemented was both efficient and effective in achieving success related to the goal, the next step is to determine whether the policy should continue as is, whether it should be altered, or whether it should be altogether done away with. It is rare that a policy remains as is. Most policies are altered in some way or another to meet changing goals. We saw this with the changes to the TPSNP instituted by the Agricultural Commissioner and the Texas Legislature earlier in the chapter. One example of how evaluation occurs in the state of Texas is through **sunset provisions**. Sunset provisions refer to when a policy, program, or agency expires on a particular date unless it is renewed by the legislature. In 1977 Texas established the Sunset Advisory Commission which examines agencies and their functions to determine whether they continue to be needed. The Sunset Commission can recommend abolishing an entire agency or make recommendations to certain agency operations. This is essentially an evaluation of an agency's performance, including policy decisions made by the agency.

Public Policy in Texas II: Health, Criminal Justice, and Immigration Policy

Health Policy

In this second section on specific public policy areas in Texas politics, we will focus on three areas of importance: (1) health policy, (2) criminal justice policy, and (3) immigration policy. In discussing these policies we will not attempt to provide a comprehensive account of all of the policies, policy actors, and policy instruments in Texas for these policy areas. Rather, we will highlight some of the important policies and policy actors as a way of illustrating the Texas policy process in those areas.

Health policy is a broad policy area that overlaps most if not all other policy areas, as we saw with the example from the beginning of the chapter on public school education policy. Unsurprisingly, the federal government and the state government both have important roles in health policy. While Medicare is administered directly by the federal government to eligible Texas citizens, other federal health programs are administered through fiscal federalism. One of the most significant policy instruments in Texas health policy is the direct provision of financial support, funded by the federal government, for health services and insurance: Medicaid, public health insurance for low-income households, and CHIP (Children's Health Insurance Program), a public health insurance program for children. The states are primarily responsible for administering these two major, national health programs, and Texas's Medicaid program was established in 1967. Along with CHIP, Medicaid as administered and serviced by the Texas Human Services Department and the Texas Health and Human Services Commission (HHSC) provides medical coverage for more than four million low-income Texans. These programs together cover half of all children in the state and two-thirds of patients in nursing homes.

These services are directly provided by private providers, who receive reimbursement from the state under special contracts. Under Governor Rick Perry, Texas opted out of the expansion of Medicaid under the Affordable Care Act (colloquially known as Obamacare). Opposing this institution was an important interest group in Texas on health policy, the Texas Health Institute, a nonpartisan advocacy group. According to the US Department of Health and Human Services, this meant that 1.1 million eligible Texans were left off of the Medicaid roles, costing low-income Texans significant health and financial gains. Opponents of the ACA, such as the Dallas-based, nonpartisan advocacy group, the National Center for Policy Analysis, point out that the expansion subsidies expire after several years, leaving the states with the unmanageable financial burden of supporting the expanded Medicaid roles in their states.

Criminal Justice Policy

Texas criminal justice policy is largely a product of the Texas criminal justice system, consisting of the state and local court system, state and local police forces, and the state and local jail and prison systems in Texas. The primary public agency responsible for criminal justice policy in Texas is the Texas Department of Criminal Justice (TDCJ). It is overseen by the Texas Board of Criminal Justice, which selects the executive director of the TDCJ. As noted earlier in the chapter, the Texas Department of Criminal Justice is the largest state employer in Texas. This is largely the case due to the fact that the TDCJ is, in addition to its other law enforcement and criminal justice mandates, responsible for staffing, supervising, and maintaining the public jails and prisons in the state of Texas and that Texas has one of the highest incarceration rates in the United States, a country with one of the highest rates in the world. Texas has more prisoners than any other state. As of 2014, Texas had 24 percent more prisoners than California, the state with the second highest prison population. Texas has 221,800 persons in prison or jail, a rate of about 1,130 per 100,000 adults, coming in at the sixth highest incarceration rate in the Union. Naturally, one of the most pressing issues in criminal justice policy are issues such as overcrowding and **recidivism**, the act of prisoners released into the general population after completing their sentence or being paroled reoffending. Critics of the Texas incarceration rate argue that the Texas "law and order" political culture yields overly harsh sentencing and overly long prison sentences, leading to overcrowding.

Texas has responded to prison overcrowding and the cost of incarceration with a unique policy instrument: **privatization**. Texas has outsourced a considerable portion of its prison population to private prisons, where prisons are run by third party corporations contracted by the government. Interest groups such as the Texas ACLU, have advocated against prison privatization citing the lack of transparency for private prisons, lack of community input, and that private prisons are thus unaccountable. Proponents cite cost savings and better performance when compared to public prisons. Some studies have shown that states can conserve considerable resources by using for-profit prisons, while others suggest the cost-savings are minimal.

Another important area of criminal justice policy is the death penalty. The TDCJ is in charge of executions in Texas. TDCJ houses death row prisoners after they are transported from their counties post-conviction, and it administers the death penalty on a condemned person's court-scheduled date of execution barring a stay issued by a Texas appellate court. A person assessed the death penalty in Texas upon conviction of a capital crime has an automatic appeal to the Texas Court of Criminal Appeals, the state's highest criminal tribunal. The TCCA examines the trial record for constitutional or procedural defects in the trial, including the sentencing phase. In addition to seeking judicial review of their sentence, death row inmates may also appeal to the Texas Board of Pardons and Paroles and request a commutation of their death sentence to life in prison. The board considers testimony and the record when rendering decisions. Texas is the national leader in executions, with one-third of all executions in the United States occurring in Texas. The TBPP determines whether or not to recommend commutation to the governor who has the ultimate authority to issue a commutation. Texas has executive 474 prisoners since the Supreme Court allowed the reinstitution of the death penalty in the 1976 case, *Greg v. Georgia*. Texas is second only to Oklahoma (25.78) in execution rate, with 13.71 executions per million (state population) being carried out by the TDCJ since 1976. As of 2011, there were 321 inmates in Texas on death row.

Like most areas of public policy, the death penalty has its critics and supporters in Texas. A pressure group opposed to the death penalty in Texas, the Texas Coalition to Abolish the Death Penalty, argues that the death penalty is bad policy and immoral. Critics, like the TCADP, also point out the high cost of the death penalty, with it costing about three times as much to executive a prisoner as to imprison someone for life. They point to the fact that thirteen individuals have been released from the Texas death row due to evidence of their wrongful conviction since 1973. Furthermore, they argue there is evidence Texas may have executed innocent persons, citing the cases of Ruben Cantu and Cameron Todd Willingham. Finally, death penalty opponents point to a number of academic studies which suggest the death penalty does not have a deterrent effect: that having the death penalty deters people from committing capital crimes. Proponents in favor of the death penalty of Texas point to the democratic mandate for the death penalty in the state: Texans remain strongly in favor of the death penalty. In a poll conducted jointly by the University of Texas and Texas Tech in 2012, 73 percent of Texans either somewhat or strongly supported the death penalty, and only 21 percent opposed it.

Immigration Policy

Immigration policy is an especially important and controversial public policy area in the state of Texas. In 2006 the US Congress sparked a national debate over illegal immigration, which has put Texas immigration policy at the forefront of the debate over immigration policy. This is complicated by the federal government's constitutional responsibility to enforce security on the national borders, which means that Texas and federal authorities are often at loggerheads over appropriate border policy and how to deal with illegal immigration. The federal government exercises plenary power in the area of border security, meaning that federal law preempts state laws that attempt to regulate immigration laws and enforcement. For example, the Supreme Court ruled in *Arizona v. United States* that a law which made it a state misdemeanor crime for an illegal immigrant to be in Arizona without documents was unconstitutional. Justice Kennedy reasoned that the federal government's authority to regulate immigration and aliens was "broad" and "undoubted" and that, since the federal government was already regulating in this area, the **doctrine of preemption** meant that state efforts to pass such laws was unconstitutional. That said, states may pass laws and institute regulations that take into account legal status, and status checks by state law enforcement were upheld in the Arizona case. Furthermore, state and federal officials often work hand-in-hand on border security and illegal immigration enforcement. While the US Border Patrol has primary responsibility for securing the border, state and local law enforcement play significant roles in deterring illegal immigration as well. The Texas Homeland Security State Administrative Agency (THSSAA), a division of the Texas Department of Public Safety, is primarily responsible for promulgating and enforcing rules and regulations related to border security and immigration in the state of Texas. The THSSAA recently instituted a new program for providing resources and paying for costs related to increased border patrols under the 2015 Local Border Security Program.

Due to the fact that Texas and Mexico share an international border, Texas is second only to California in the number of undocumented immigrants living in the state. According to the Department of Homeland Security, as of 2009, 1.68 million undocumented immigrants were living in Texas. The recent border crisis related to thousands of children, originating from countries in Latin America and South America experiencing economic and political strife, crossing the Texas border illegally in 2014 has led to both administrative and legislative responses that significantly impact immigration policy in Texas. Texas Governor Rick Perry sent 1,000 National Guard troops to help secure the border in response to the border crisis in the Rio Grande Valley. In the 84th session of the Texas Legislature, a number of laws affecting border security and immigration policy were passed and signed into law. Governor Greg Abbot, citing Mexican drug cartel activity on the border, signed into law a border security bill that spends millions of dollars to bolster the ranks of state police operating on the Texas–Mexico border and increased investment in border technology. In response to President Obama's executive order to halt deportations for as many as five million undocumented immigrants, Governor Abbot signed a law mandating the use of E-Verify, a software program that compares employee documents to US government records in order to determine if the employee is eligible to work in the United States in all state agencies and higher education institutions. Concerned about undocumented immigrants participating in Texas elections, Texas passed a Voter ID law in 2011 that required voters to show a photo ID in order to vote, and it was upheld by the US Supreme Court.

Immigration and border security policy in Texas is politically controversial, with organized groups and political groups on either side of the issue. Hot topics like amnesty legislation (laws designed to give current illegal immigrants in the country a path toward legal status), **sanctuary cities** (cities with laws forbidding local law enforcement from participating in deportation and border security actions) deportation, border fencing, border patrols, the threat of terrorism and crime on and across the border, and voting rights are all salient and strongly contested political issues related to immigration policy in Texas. Those who support strict immigration laws, E-Verify and Voter ID, and advocate for strong border security argue that the state pays too much to provide services to illegal immigrants. Anti-illegal immigrant activists argue that undocumented immigrants are not required to pay taxes and thus support these services, as citizens are required to do. Groups like the Minuteman Project, NumbersUSA, and the Center for Immigration Studies argue that illegal immigration contributes to greater crime, makes the country more vulnerable to terrorist threats, and represents an unfair source of competition for American jobs. While groups like the Mexican American Legal Defense and Educational Fund, the National Council of La Raza, Texas, and the Reform Immigration for Texas Alliance argue that anti-illegal immigrant policies are unfair, racially discriminatory, and ignore the critical role that immigrants play in the Texas economy, particularly in the agricultural and service industries. They argue policies like E-Verify and Voter ID laws are racially discriminatory and discourage companies from locating to Texas and hurts existing Texas businesses. There is little question that immigration policy will continue to be at the forefront of both national and Texas politics for the foreseeable future.

Conclusion: Policy Innovations and Public Policy in Twenty-First-Century Texas

The Texas public policy environment is a complex, integrated, and institutionally diverse setting for policymaking in the gamut of political issue areas. As we have seen, new and innovative policies are being formulated, implemented, and evaluated through the use of traditional and unique policy instruments to address important and salient public problems in Texas. In the twenty-first-century Texas economy, innovations in health policy and forays into fiscal federalism, like the Affordable Care Act, require Texas policy institutions and policymakers to evolve and adjust their policy instruments to account for top-down changes in the policy environment. While citizen activists and interest groups call for status quo-altering policy changes in areas like immigration and criminal justice policy, policy actors continue to push the envelope in state policymaking and adopt rules, regulations, and requirements that are at the cutting edge of state, local, and national politics. As the policy environment continues to evolve over time, it will be essential that Texas policymakers effectively and efficiently diagnose public problems and adopt and implement policies that address these problems in service to the people of Texas.

Key Terms

fiscal federalism
subgovernments
discretion
block grants
policy stages heuristic (PSH)
policy cycle
Garbage Can Model
policy window
policy entrepreneurs
policy network
policy diffusion
policy stakeholders
boards and commissions

bounded rationality
sunset provisions
subsidies
recidivism
privatization
doctrine of preemption
sanctuary cities

References

Aguilar, Julian. "Abbot Signs Bill Mandating Use of E-Verify." *The Texas Tribune*, June 10, 2015.

———. "Abbot Signs Sweeping Border Security Bill." *The Texas Tribune*, June 9, 2015.

———. "Tribpedia: Immigration." *The Texas Tribune*, July 22, 2015.

Ansell, Christopher K. *Pragmatist Democracy: Evolutionary Learning as Public Philosophy*. Oxford University Press, 2011.

Arizona v. United States, 567 United States Reporter _____ (2012).

Boen, Hannah. "Local Public Schools Adhere to Strict Nutrition Policies: 21k Balanced Meals Are No Piece of Cake." *Abilene Reporter-News*, September 12, 2011.

Camarota, Steven A. "Immigration and Terrorism." news release, October 12, 2001, 2001, http://cis.org/ImmigrationPolicy%2526Terrorism.

Carey, Isiah. "Audit Reveals Some Houston Schools Violating Nutrition Guidelines." *FOX-Houston*, March 25, 2013.

Carson, David. "Texas Execution Primer." Texas Execution Information Center, http://www.txexecutions.org/primer.asp.

Cullen, Karen W., and Kathleen B. Watson. "The Impact of the Texas Public School Nutrition Policy on Student Food Selection and Sales in Texas." *American Journal of Public Health* 99, no. 4 (April, 2009): 706–12.

deLeon, Peter. "The Stages Approach to the Policy Process: What Has It Done? Where Is It Going?". In *Theories of the Policy Process*, edited by Paul A. Sabatier. Theoretical Lenses on Public Policy. Boulder, CO: Westview Press, 1999.

DePrang, Emily. "More Prisoners, More Problems: Mass Incarceration Climbs Again." *Texas Observer*, September 17, 2014.

Dickman, Sam, David Himmelstein, Danny McCormick, and Steffie Woolhandler. "Opting out of Medicaid Expansion: The Health and Financial Impacts." healthaffairs.org, http://healthaffairs.org/blog/2014/01/30/opting-out-of-medicaid-expansion-the-health-and-financial-impacts/.

Glaze, Lauren E., and Danielle Kaeble. "Correctional Populations in the United States, 2013." Washington, D.C.: Bureau of Justice Statistics (BJS), 2014.

Gregg v. Georgia, 428 United States Reports 153 (1976).

Hammond, Bill. "Rejecting Keystone Xl Is a Mistake." news release, January, 18 2012, 2012, http://www.txbiz.org/news/newsarticledisplay.aspx?ArticleID=25.

Hennessy-Fiske, Molly. "Texas Gov. Rick Perry Order 1,000 National Guard Troops to Border." *Los Angeles Times*, July 21, 2014.

Herrick, Devon. "Medicaide Expansion Will Bankrupt the States." West, Allen, http://www.ncpa.org/pub/ba729.

Hershaw, Eva. "Heated Debate Surrounds Push for Deep Fryers in Schools." *The Texas Tribune*, April 24, 2015.

Higgins, Fred. "Implementation of the Texas Public School Nutrition Policy." Austin, TX: Texas Department of Agriculture, 2010.

Howlett, Michael, and M. Ramesh. *Studying Public Policy: Policy Cycles and Policy Subsystems*. 2nd ed. New York, NY: Oxford University Press, 2003.

Huber, John D., and Charles R. Shipan. *Deliberate Discretion? The Institutional Foundations of Bureaucratic Autonomy*. Cambridge Studies in Comparative Politics. Edited by Margaret Levi New York, NY: Cambridge University Press, 2002.

Janek, Kyle L., Chris Traylor, and Kay Ghahremani. *Texas Medicaid and Chip in Perspective*. Tenth ed. Austin, TX: Texas Health and Human Services Commission, 2015.

Jervis, Rick. "Controversial Texas Textbooks Headed to Classrooms." *USA Today*, November 17, 2014.

Johnson, Kevin R. "Race, the Immigration Laws, and Domstice Race Relations: A "Magic Mirror" into the Heart of Darkness." *Indiana Law Journal* 73 (Fall, 1998): 1111–59.

Kever, Jeannie. "Commission Refuses to Be Derailed: Revamp and Name Change to Reflect Energy Mission Fall by the Wayside." *Houston Chronicle*, May 16, 2013.

King, Ken. "Bill Analysis: H.B. 1781." Texas State Legislature, http://www.legis.state.tx.us/tlodocs/83R/analysis/html/HB01781H.HTM.

Lasswell, Harold D. "The Policy Orientation." In *The Policy Sciences: Recent Developments in Scope and Method*, edited by Daniel Lerner and Harold D. Lasswell. Stanford, California: Stanford University Press, 1951.

Lewis, Matt K. "Does Illegal Immigration Cost Jobs? (a Debate)." *The Daily Caller*, March 31, 2015.

Liptak, Adam. "Supreme Court Allows Texas to Use Strict Voter ID Law in Coming Election." *The New York Times*, October 19, 2014, A19.

Lohan, Tara. "The Keystone Xl Pipeline's 'Accidental Activists'." Moyers & Company, http://billmoyers.com/2014/01/22/how-obama-threw-the-south-under-a-bus-for-the-keystone-xl-pipeline/.

Lombardo, Crystal. "Top 4 Pros and Cons of Private Prisons." National Latino Council on Alcohol and Tobacco Prevention, http://nlcatp.org/top-4-pros-and-cons-of-private-prisons/.

McGee, Kate. "Fried Food in School Cafeterias: 'It's About Freedom and Liberty,' Says Ag Commissioner." KUT.org, http://kut.org/post/fried-food-school-cafeterias-its-about-freedom-and-liberty-says-ag-commissioner.

Mendoza, Jason A., Kathleen B. Watson, and Karen W. Cullen. "Change in Dietary Energy Density after Implementation of the Texas Public School Nutrition Policy." *Journal of the American Diet Association* 110, no. 3 (March, 2010): 434–40.

Nowrasteh, Alex. "E-Verify's Slippery Slope." *The Hill*, March 10, 2015.

Oppel Jr., Richard A. "Private Prisons Found to Offer Little in Savings." *The New York Times*, May 19, 2011, A1.

Ortiz, Ildefonso. "Drug Cartels Turn Illegal Immigrants Quest for the American Dream into a Nightmare." *Breitbart News*, October 12, 2014.

Peters, B. Guy. *American Public Policy: Promise and Performance*. Los Angeles, CA: Sage, 2013.

Prindle, David F. *Petroleum Politics and the Texas Railroad Commission*. Austin, TX: University of Texas Press, 1981.

Ramsey, Ross. "Ut/Tt Poll: Texans Stand Behind Death Penalty." *The Texas Tribune*, May 24, 2012.

Rogers, Simon. "Death Penalty Statistics from the USs: Which State Executes the Most People?" *The Guardian*, September 21, 2011.

Rosenfeld, Steven. "12 Reasons Texas' New Voter ID Law Is Racist." *Salon*, October 21, 2014.

Sabatier, Paul A. "The Need for Better Theories." In *Theories of the Policy Process*, edited by Paul A. Sabatier. Theoretical Lenses on Public Policy. Boulder, CO: Westview Press, 2015.

———, ed. *Theories of the Policy Process*. Edited by Paul A. Sabatier, Theoretical Lenses on Public Policy. Boulder, CO: Westview Press, 1999.

Sabatier, Paul A., and Hank C. Jenkins-Smith, eds. *Policy Change and Learning: An Advocacy Coalition Approach*. Edited by Paul A. Sabatier, Theoretical Lenses on Public Policy. Boulder, CO: Westview Press, 1993.

Salamon, Jeff. "Everything You Ever Wanted to Know About Illegal Immigration (but Didn't Know Who to Ask)." *Texas Monthly*, 2010.

Shughart, William F., Robert D. Tolison, and Zhipeng Yan. "Rent Seeking into the Income Distribution." *Kyklos* 56 (2003): 441–56.

Simon, Herbert. "A Behavioral Model of Rational Choice." In *Models of Man, Social and Rational: Mathematical Essays on Rational Human Behavior in a Social Setting*, edited by Herbert A. Simon. New York, NY: Wiley, 1957.

Simpson, Matt. "A Win for Texas: Proposed Limits on Investment by Judges in for-Profit Prisons." ACLU, http://www.aclutx.org/blog/?cat=40.

Smith, Morgan. "In Education Reform Debate, One Group Stands Out." *The Texas Tribune*, May 12, 2013.

Staff. "Public Citizen Calls for Probe of Construction Problems on Keystone Xl Southern Segment: Startup Should Be Delayed to Ensure Pipeline Saftey." news release, November 19, 2013, http://www.citizen.org/pressroom/pressroomredirect.cfm?ID=4028.

TAH. "The State of Obesity in Texas." Robert Wood Johnson Foundation, http://stateofobesity.org/states/tx/.

TCADP. "Texas Death Penalty Facts." Texas Coalition to Abolish the Death Penalty, http://tcadp.org/get-informed/texas-death-penalty-facts/.

TCEQ. "Mission Statement and Agency Philosophy." Texas Commision on Environmental Quality, http://www.tceq.state.tx.us/about/mission.html.

TDAFN. "Texas Public School Nutrition Policy." edited by Food and Nutrition Division Texas Department of Agriculture. Austin, TX: Texas Department of Agricluture, 2005.

THI. "Health Care Reform." Texas Health Institute, http://www.texashealthinstitute.org/health-care-reform.html.

Thomas, Clive S., and Ronald J. Hrebenar. "Interest Group Power in the Fifty States: Trends since the Late 1970s." *Comparative State Politics* 20 (1999): 3–17.

THSSAA. "2015 Local Border Security Program." Texas Department of Public Saftey, https://www.txdps.state.tx.us/director_staff/saa/2015LBSPGrantInfo.htm.

TRAIL. "Trail List of Texas State Agencies." Texas State Library and Archives Commission, https://www.tsl.texas.gov/apps/lrs/agencies/index.html.

TSAC. "Frequently Asked Questions." Texas Sunset Advisory Commission, https://www.sunset.texas.gov/about-us/frequently-asked-questions.

Zuckerman, Mortimer. "Harsh Sentencing, Overstuffed Prisons-It's Time for Reform." *The Wall Street Journal*, May 2, 2014.

Exercise 7.1 ■ Multiple Choice

1. Which of the following represents a way that states have wide latitude in interpreting and implementing policy within federal programs?
   a. Categorical grants
   b. Block grants
   c. Discretionary federalism
   d. Subgovernmental contracts

2. During which step of Lasswell's policy stages heuristic would the Texas Commission on Environmental Quality publicize a policy on its website and publish a report that analyzed the requirements of the policy?
   a. Policy Agenda Setting and Problem Definition
   b. Policy Formulation
   c. Policy Adoption
   d. Policy Implementation
   e. Policy Evaluation

3. John Smith owns a piece of property in Texas which was taken by the government through the power of eminent domain in order to construct a new highway. Mr. Smith decides to speak out against the taking of his property and against the construction of the highway which he believes will disrupt the community. John Smith is acting as a(n):
   a. Citizen activist
   b. Interest group
   c. Elected official
   d. None of the above

4. When a policy decision-maker must make a decision but is limited by time, knowledge, and skills, that policymaker is using what type of rationality?
   a. Controlled rationality
   b. Decisional rationality
   c. Constructed rationality
   d. Bounded rationality

5. What difficulty can occur when multiple organizations are tasked with implementing a public policy but no single agency is in control?
   a. Accountability
   b. Formulation
   c. Evaluation
   d. Monitoring

6. Under House Bill 40, Governor Abbott gave which governmental entity power over fracking policy?
   a. Municipalities
   b. Independent districts
   c. Townships
   d. State government

7. Which Texas agency is tasked with the responsibility of ensuring that air quality meets required standards?
   a. Texas Commission on Air Quality
   b. Texas Commission on Environmental Quality
   c. Texas Clean Air Agency
   d. Texas Environmental Protection Agency

8. Which program did Texas opt out of while under the term of Governor Rick Perry?
   a. Expansion of Medicare
   b. Expansion of Medicaid
   c. Expansion of CHIP
   d. All of the above

9. What is it called when the government contracts with a third party corporation for the purpose of running a prison?
   a. Parolization
   b. Commutation
   c. Grantmaking
   d. None of the above

10. Which of the following agencies is primarily responsible for promulgating and enforcing rules and regulations related to border security and immigration in the state of Texas?
    a. Texas Border Control Agency
    b. Texas Agency on Immigration Affairs
    c. Texas Homeland Security State Administrative Agency
    d. Texas Department of Homeland Border Control

Exercise 7.2   ■   Research Exercise

Several states in the US including Colorado, Washington, Oregon, and Alaska have passed laws allowing for the legalization of small amounts of marijuana. This signals a shift in the drug policies of those particular states. For this exercise, find and discuss one article that discusses the advantages and one article that discusses the disadvantages of this change in drug policy. Be sure the articles focus on the policy and are from reputable sources. Present an argument as to whether the state of Texas should change its policy regarding marijuana (which is not legalized in the state, except for medical marijuana in limited circumstances). Be sure to provide the full citations for the articles.

Exercise 7.3　■　Writing Exercise

If you were responsible for developing an energy policy for Texas, what would the policy look like? How much would you rely on traditional non-renewable resources? How much on non-traditional, renewable resources? Be sure to be realistic and consider the pros and cons of all sources, meaning who would be for and against your plan and would it be likely get passed. Your response should be a minimum of one page and be sure to include an introduction, conclusion, and a list of any sources that you use.

9 781524 922481